Praise

'An outstanding attitude and what a role model Liv is.'

— **Karren Brady** CBE

'I think Liv Conlon is reason enough to be so hopeful about the future. A young business leader with both entrepreneurial savvy and a strong commitment to purpose and contribution to society; she's just the young leader the world needs. I've no doubt this book will impact all who read it.'

— **Jessica Huie MBE**, Author of *Purpose*

'Liv's book is the step-by-step guide that I wish I had when I was starting out.'

— **Marc Randolph**, Co-Founder of Netflix

'Liv is an inspiration to everyone, regardless of age. Her work ethic is impeccable and I am constantly impressed by her creativity. She is a real beacon of hope for anyone looking for the motivation to take their future into their own hands and launch a business. Not only is her journey incredible but she gives you the blueprint to blaze your own trail on the entrepreneurial voyage.'

— **Mike Handcock,** Chairman of The Circle of Excellence Group

Too Big For Your Boots

How I Built a **7-figure** Brand
as a Young Entrepreneur
with No Startup Funds
and No Experience

Liv Conlon

Rᵉthink

First published in Great Britain in 2021 by Rethink Press
(www.rethinkpress.com)

Cover image © Julie Lamont Photography,
www.julielamont.co.uk

*For my brother Jack, who has always
encouraged me to reach for the moon,
and my mum, who has always been my guiding star.
Without you both, this book wouldn't have been possible.*

Contents

Foreword

By Netflix Co-Founder, Marc Randolph

Follow your dreams!

Anyone who has ever sat through a university commencement speech has heard that one before. In fact, it's probably the most dispensed piece of advice ever. Adam probably told it to Eve, and it's been trotted out ever since by graduation speakers, by teachers and parents, and in an endless stream of self-help books, greetings cards and social media posts.

But you know what's funny? No one ever gets around to telling you how. There is no class at school called 'Follow Your Dreams 101'. And last I looked, there's no book called *Following Your Dreams For Dummies*.

At least there wasn't until now. As soon as I picked up an early draft of Liv's book, I realised that this is something special. Although she has had a crazy amount of success for someone her age, this isn't the typical business autobiography laying out in excruciating detail how great she is. This is something different. This is about her failures as much as her successes. It explains not only how she did it, but breaks down in detail all the steps that anyone else could take to make their dreams a reality. This is her effort to give back.

It certainly resonates with me. Twenty-two years ago I was a thirty-three-year-old father of three, out of work, with a simple dream: I just wanted to start a company that sold something on the internet. And I had plenty of big ideas. One of them was personalised shampoo! I was going to have people cut off locks of their hair and mail it to my team of ace hair scientists who would formulate a custom shampoo just for them!

Don't like it? OK, how about this one, then: custom dog food! Let us know all about your dog: their breed, gender, age, activity level – even what climate they live in – and we will formulate a custom dog food just for them.

Don't like that one either? OK. How about DVD rental by mail? Crazy idea, right?

Well, as implausible as it may sound now, that's the one we chose. And after six months of raising money, putting together a team, building a simple website, making sure we had every DVD available, and struggling to find some way to promote it, in April of 1998 I finally got to launch that company and see my dream become a reality. Oh, and I probably should tell you what we named that little company. We called it Netflix.

That was twenty-two years ago, and although Netflix is now the largest entertainment streaming company in the world, with nearly 200 million subscribers, I promise you that at the beginning it was no different than the dream you might have. We were small. We struggled. We couldn't afford furniture so we used folding tables for desks, and I brought in the family beach chairs to sit in. We were always short of money, and almost went out of business countless times.

But what makes the Netflix story different than so many dreams is that I did the most important thing that any dreamer can do. I started.

Like Liv, I didn't know what I was doing, but like her, I was confident I could figure it out. I promise that you can too. The fact that you're holding this book in your hands means you've already taken your first steps. And reading it will put you in a better position to be successful than I ever was.

Liv's book is that step-by-step guide that I wish I had when I was starting out. Whether it's coming up with your idea and getting the courage to start, or taking an existing business and learning how to bring it to the next level, Liv provides detailed advice and encouragement drawn from her own experiences of starting and growing her business.

It's all there: finding your first clients; branding your business; launching it to the public; mastering social media and content marketing – all illustrated with Liv's honest insights and heartfelt encouragement.

This is not just a book for entrepreneurs. Its lessons are applicable for anyone with a dream, whether that be doing something not-for-profit, starting a club, getting a better job or just wanting a better life for yourself. The lessons here are universal.

And I promise: anyone can do it. In the last fifteen years I've worked with thousands of young entrepreneurs on every continent, in small towns, big cities and everything in between. I've learned that you don't need certain skills or a specific education. One of my favourite entrepreneurs dropped out of their university, drove an ambulance in Los Angeles for several years, fought forest fires in Montana, and then started his own company. Another started her own company after playing in a ska band for ten years (with dreads below her waist). Another is only seventeen years old.

I'm not saying it's easy. It takes a tolerance for risk. It takes hard work, persistence, passion and resilience. It takes confidence. But taking on something hard and succeeding is one of the greatest joys in life. And you'll never know what your dream might have become if you don't try it.

So go ahead and turn off Netflix for a few hours. (It's OK. I won't mind.) Turn off your phone and leave

Instagram for tomorrow. Find a comfortable chair and start reading. Make notes. Try things. Experiment.

In the pages ahead you're going to share in Liv's struggles and her triumphs. You're going to laugh and cry. You're certainly going to learn a lot. But (and I'm sure Liv will agree with me here)...reading a book is... well...just reading a book.

So, when you're done, I need you to take the biggest and hardest step of all. I need you to put the book down, screw up your nerve and just start. Take that first step to start turning your dream into a reality. Without taking that first step, you'll never get anywhere. But you'll see...once you're underway making your own dreams come true, there's not a better experience in the world.

Good luck,

Marc

Marc Randolph is the co-founder and first CEO of Netflix, and the author of *That Will Never Work: The Birth Of Netflix And The Amazing Life Of An Idea.*

1
My Story

Let's begin by being completely honest with each other. I have no idea how to start a book, just like I had no clue how to start a business when I was sixteen. I started anyway and I managed to scale that business to a yearly turnover of £1 million by the time I was nineteen. You don't need to know everything before you start – just start. I wasn't given a step-by-step manual on how to get here. I didn't have life experience or knowledge. It wasn't an accident. I built a £1-million brand in my teens but I didn't have *How To Build A Seven-Figure Business By Nineteen For Dummies*. How I wish I had.

But, hey, I got there. I want to get a few things clear upfront with you before we dive in. I'm going to be transparent about what it's like to build a business at a young age, sharing the good, the bad and the ugly. I'm going to be honest about the big mistakes I've made and also share the big wins, in the hope that I fast-track your success and you learn from some of my lessons. However, consider this a warning before you read any further: if you're looking for a sugar-coated narrative surrounding being your own boss, this isn't the book for you.

Behind the perceived glitz and glamour of being an entrepreneur and being part of the massive #GirlBoss movement, the reality is different to what you think may be involved. The sassy and stylish Instagram feed is a rose-tinted view of what it takes to become a true entrepreneur. The award ceremonies, the interviews and the social media following are wonderful; however, it can conceal the exhaustion of running a business.

Making your way to the top is a culmination of hard work and dedication. Becoming an entrepreneur really epitomises the saying 'blood, sweat and tears'. Well, maybe not the blood (in my case at least). The real journey will not be a Pinterest-worthy photo feed. To make it to the top you will need to sacrifice life as you know it, but in my experience it's completely worth it.

Starting out in business at sixteen, I have made a lot of sacrifices to follow my dreams and live my passion. People say that I missed out on a lot of the fun of being a regular teenager, which is absolutely true, but

I have never regretted following my true purpose. It's important for those of you starting out on your entrepreneurial journey to truly know the sacrifices required. Are you in?

Great! In order for you to get a sense of what it takes to become a successful young entrepreneur, I'm going to share my journey with you, from the first business I started at thirteen to where I am today. Everyone's entrepreneurial journey starts differently. Maybe yours will start by reading this book (one can hope). Here's my story.

The Very Beginning

You know that feeling you get when you just don't belong? Given you are reading this book, I'm assuming you do, because it's not 'normal' to want to start a business at our age... or so they tell us. I first realised I was different when I attended high school. Playing video games, going to sleepovers and talking incessantly about boys just didn't float my boat. I went to bed every night at 9pm and woke up at 4am to 'seize the day' and not much has changed since. I hated school, even though I was pretty good at most subjects. I was that person in the class who would question how anything we were learning was relevant to everyday life. To this day I have never used Pythagoras' Theorem. I was never the skinniest or the prettiest girl at school; I felt tall and awkward. I was the girl who was just one of the boys. The other girls never understood and I refused to be who I 'should' be.

Can you tell already that I'm not very compliant? When I'm told I 'should' do something, I naturally do the exact opposite. This wasn't me trying to be awkward or different, I just was. I hated the school bell signifying that I 'should' be hungry enough to eat lunch for the next hour, or learning a subject because someone once said that's what teenagers 'should' be studying. Now? I eat lunch when I choose or, heck, I can have two lunches. I wake up when I choose. I finish work when I choose. I choose who I work with. I choose what I do every day. I guess the writing was on the wall. I was always going to be my own boss. I'm incapable of following the 'rules'.

My First Business

My first step to becoming my own boss began when I launched a business at thirteen. I had been buying fake nails from my local pharmacy, which retailed at £9.99. Even at thirteen, each time I handed over my hard-earned pocket money I felt ripped off. I was spending my money on something that would last five days, if I was lucky. Lots of girls my age were buying them too. This shop was making a lot of dough selling crappy plastic nails that were made in China. Thinking back as I write, I was kind of a badass (as far as thirteen-year-old entrepreneurs go). I researched whether I could import them from China and discovered I could. The answer was the website Alibaba.

I could buy the exact same product for £0.38. This was my first ever lightbulb moment in business, and we'll talk more about that in Chapter 3. I had been paying an extra £9.61 for the exact same product. They say the best business ideas are born out of frustration, and my business idea was no different. The minimum order was, of course, 500 packs. It was an ambitious amount to shift, but at thirteen you have little inhibition. I started to work double time around the house, picking up any extra chores I could from my parents, and came up with the £190 I needed to make the minimum order. I decided on a £4.99 price point, undercutting the high street stores by 50% to capture both people I knew and online purchasers. The order arrived, I unpacked it and before long I had made my first online sale, on 25 August 2011, to a woman in West Yorkshire, England.

My main sales strategy was to do business online with eBay and at market stalls throughout Glasgow. I quickly realised that, in business, you don't often create a product that people *Instantly* want to buy. It took time, hard work and hustle to sell my first 500 packs. It's never as quick or as easy as you think. There were days I lost money, willpower and hope. I spent hours freezing at markets in the winter, punting my nails as Christmas gifts. It wasn't as picturesque as you might think. I wasn't in New York's Rockefeller Center but in an alley just off Glasgow's Buchanan Street, which is a sight for sore eyes only on the sunniest of days. If you have any knowledge of the Scottish climate, you'll know they don't come around often and they certainly never came around when I was selling my wares.

One day it was -2°C and the rain was destroying my little stall. The bunting I had spent hours making was blown away, and I lost days afterwards due to the chill that ran right through me and resulted with me in bed with a cold. I sold two packets that day, making sales of £9.98. Having paid £150 to rent the stall, I made a loss of £140.02 and a little bit of my enthusiasm. However, I got out of bed and did it again and again. I wasn't going to let a small bump in the road stop me. This level of determination would serve me well in future.

My school side hustle became a catalyst for me. It proved to me that this is what I wanted to do, although I realised it was a lot harder than I initially anticipated. It wasn't as easy as popping something up on the internet and making thousands or putting a sign up at a stall and selling hundreds, but I liked the challenge. That's what we entrepreneurs have in common: we are problem solvers. The world presents us with a problem and we work out how to fix it or how to make something better. I felt impassioned, for the first time in a long time, with something that mattered to me. I began to enjoy the rush of a sale when I heard the laptop ping – another order to fulfil. I enjoyed the delight I felt when someone approached my stall and bought the three-for-two offer. I enjoyed the feeling of no longer hoovering the car for some pocket money. At thirteen, I was already learning I didn't want to sell my time for cash.

A Passion For Business

My mum, self-employed at the time, got involved when I needed an adult. She joined me on days at the stall and accompanied me to the post office to send my orders. She has been there through it all, freezing with me on the streets of Glasgow to lavish dinners at 10 Downing Street. I told her I'd pay her back one day. During our time at the stall she noticed how dedicated to the business I was and how much I was loving the world of entrepreneurship. She recalls that she had never seen me so happy. Entrepreneurship was my drug, and oh, boy, was I hooked.

I was obsessed with business and I was craving to know more. If business was a door, I had only taken a small peep through the keyhole thus far. I wanted to open that door wide and explore every inch of the world behind it. My mum invited me to join her at business meetings and networking events, and to go away with her on business trips. I was the youngest person at every event and I was known as 'Ali's daughter'. Funnily enough, when Mum and I attend events now, she's known as 'Liv's mum'. Oh, how the tables have turned. She finds it hysterical.

My mum has always been my biggest inspiration and supporter in business. She is an independent woman (cue the Destiny's Child hit), and she often worked long hours and away from home. However, she got to work from nice hotels, meeting other successful business owners. On those trips, ditching many school days to get my real schooling in business, I fell in love with the shiny rewards that I believed entrepreneurship would instantly give me. I may have entered into the property industry with those rose-tinted specs on but I was ready for whatever the world had to throw at me, and it threw me many a curveball. The first properties I staged were on Glasgow streets where you wouldn't want to leave your car unattended.

I loved every second of running the eBay store, and I re-invested the money I made back into the business at fourteen, buying my first MacBook. I had caught the bug. Business was an escape from what was going on behind the scenes at school. They say that your school days are the best of your life; unfortunately for me it was quite the opposite. My school life felt like a never-ending black hole that I was sent to every day and I couldn't see the light at the end of the tunnel. They were the hardest years of my life so far. From ages five to sixteen I *Never* fit in. The bullying started at high school.

The Catalyst

It's easy to look back on the years of being bullied as a blessing now – they shaped me into who I am today and drove me to the success I now enjoy. At the time it was extremely difficult. It was a period of my life when I felt hopeless. I think there is often a misconception that only quiet and frail people are bullied. There were people I knew who were like that, but I was the opposite. I was outgoing, good at sports and got A grades in all of my subjects. I shone too brightly and certain people took umbrage with that. The insight I'm about to give you about my experience at school is a theme that has run throughout my entire life.

As time passed I tried to ignore those around me and what was going on in my school life by launching myself into my business. As my grades got better, their voices got louder. The tactics to strip me of any confidence got more brutal, painful and insidious. I masked what was really going on. No one would have guessed someone like me was being bullied. When I left class and no longer had the safety blanket of a teacher present the bullies would humiliate me on social media or on their group chat. It felt like I was in a glass room with no holes for air. You could see me from the outside, I appeared fine, but as I started to lose oxygen I felt I had nowhere to go and developed an inability to breathe.

With my oxygen tank running on low for so long, I broke. I couldn't take it any longer. I decided enough was enough. I went home, I internalised the situation for forty-eight hours and then told my parents what had been happening. They were shocked and upset but hugely supportive. Until then I had presented the perfect exterior – I was top of my class, I had won awards at school and I had a couple of close friends. From the outside looking in, I was flying. Internally I was drowning and I didn't know if I could continue. With my parents' support and blessing, I moved to a different school. It was the fresh start I needed, and I distanced myself physically and online from the bullies. My final year in my new school was great – no one took any notice of me and I managed to complete and graduate my final year of high school with the A grades I needed to do anything I wanted at university.

My First Win

Starting your own business is a scary path to take at sixteen. Going to university was a ticket to live at home, get a part-time job and take four years to discover what it was I really wanted to do. Being who I was, I chose the other route. I had just won a competition and I'm very competitive. It was a local Young Entrepreneur Apprentice Competition, based on the US TV programme headed by Donald Trump and the UK version headed by Alan Sugar.[1] I took part in

---

1   *The Apprentice* [US TV series] (NBC, 2004–2017); *The Apprentice* [UK TV series] (BBC Two/BBC One, 2005–present)

various business tasks over the space of two weeks, competing with sixteen other teens. And I won! It was a lot more draining and cut-throat than you would imagine; everything you've seen on TV happened in the competition. Candidates stealing other people's ideas, taking credit for things they hadn't done, and a lot of arguments. I didn't sleep or eat much during those two weeks due to overwhelming nerves. It turned into a crash course in human psychology and I learned a lot about what people are willing to do to win. I vowed that I didn't want to work with people in that capacity again, and I didn't. When they called my name as the winner of the competition I burst into tears. The stress had finally subsided and, in that moment, I knew I was truly meant to be an entrepreneur.

I was ready to march into school to tell them I'd found my destiny. I remember the day they called me into the careers office. I couldn't believe that a careers office even existed...wasn't that just in the movies? They knew that I would not be returning for my final year and I would not be applying for any universities. They were horrified and couldn't believe I was leaving with the intention of starting a home staging business. Their exact words: 'A girl like you should be going to university and then should get a real job. I think you are going to ruin your life.'

They 'shoulded' all over me again. Those words still echo in my head, even to this day. A 'real job' – what is that? Are you only successful if you become a doctor or a lawyer? Is starting your own business and building the life of your dreams not a feasible, attractive career path? The antiquated school system needs to see entrepreneurship as a possible path to success. I have been corrected for using the term 'success' when describing entrepreneurship before, as entrepreneurship doesn't prove to be a successful path for everyone. I understand that. It's one of the hardest career paths and the majority of people aren't up for the challenge. I knew that it was my destiny, so their words had a minimal impact on me, and if anything encouraged me, but for those who are willing to dip their toes in the entrepreneurial waters it might have been the one thing that stopped the next Steve Jobs. I'm working on changing that.

Beginning In Business

I'd love to tell you that I immediately left school and started my business, but I spent some time thinking and then a few weeks later I started attending property networking events. That's when I met 'John'. He had spotted my ambition and offered me a job working at his mortgage company. I would work there during the day and they would help me become a qualified mortgage advisor if I studied at night. I laugh now – can you imagine me as a mortgage advisor? Snooze button, please. No offence to mortgage advisors but it's not for me. At the time I was flattered, however, and I got caught up in it. Why, when you picture an office, do you imagine a swanky glass office, like one of those ones you see on TV, with the New York skyline in the background, men in designer suits, women in Louboutins and young professionals climbing the ladder? That was the way I pictured it so I set about purchasing some cute desk accessories for my office.

Reality check: my swanky New York dream was immediately crushed as I was faced with an old-fashioned office with dark, depressing panelled walls and a carpet older than me. There was no Harvey Spector or Donna Paulsen at the desk next to me. Oh, and I lived in Glasgow. I felt that harsh reality the minute I boarded the twenty-three-minute train ride into town. All the passengers wore dreary expressions. They looked like they were heading to be executed and I looked like a drowned rat by the time I got to the office, as my blonde curls had been ruined by the pelting rain. I ploughed on – I could do this. This was the financial security and network I needed to start building my true passion: my home staging business.

My resolve didn't last long. Three days in and I realised I couldn't do it. I made my escape at lunch, putting as much distance between myself and the office as possible. I went to a local upmarket shopping mall where I witnessed 'free' people with their friends, chatting, laughing and drinking martinis. I ran to the bathroom and burst into tears, realising this was not the life of my dreams. I wasn't going to sit in a wood-panelled office for the next few years of my life; I couldn't live like this for another second. I know this sounds like a first world problem and an entitled, petty thing to get upset over, but I felt an overwhelming sense of being trapped. When I got back I made an appointment to speak with my manager. The next morning, I resigned. It is at times like these that we realise what is truly important to us. I had been given a salary that a sixteen-year-old could only dream of but it just wasn't for me. I left my job of two days and that was the end of being 'employed'. I was never paid so I don't think it really counts.

What was next? The biggest roller coaster ride of my life.

2
Methodology

Writing a book has always been on the cards for me. Is that the right term? I must warn you, I'm bad at getting sayings right (or good at getting them wrong). Regardless, I feel that right here, right now as I write this book is exactly where I'm meant to be. I'm not going to become all spiritual on you here, as that isn't me, but I am a strong believer in the idea that 'where you are is where you're meant to be'. Which is a pretty strange thing for me to say.

With every step of my journey there has been a constant question regarding how to get to the next milestone as quickly as possible. As I gain more experience (damn those who have said that to me over the years, like my mum – they were right) I've learned to put in the work, take the action required to get there, but also hang back just a little, as things will work out the way they are meant to. This, you may be able to tell, is a reminder to take it easy – it will come. I know you want to conquer the world by a silly age, as I did, but if it's written in the stars for you then I know you're going to make it happen. I think I got that saying right this time.

Back to the point I intended to write about. This book has always been a goal and a dream of mine. I have always been clear on the *Exact* book I'd like to write and for who. That's you, by the way. I built a seven-figure business by the time I was nineteen with the odds against me. I was young, with no investment funds, no experience and no degree. 'May the odds be ever in your favour' – thanks, *Hunger Games*.[2] I'm aware, however, that I am not the only person at this age capable of doing this and I want to enable more. There is no manual on how to do this, so I thought I would write it myself. I know what I said above but come on, we have got big goals and short timescales as ambitious young entrepreneurs.

I started to document and track everything I was doing successfully (and unsuccessfully) to build a £1-million business (although I didn't know it would be at the time). There is a lot of information stored in this head of mine, and I want to share it with you. I also have been through some tough times that could have destroyed

---

2   S Collins, *The Hunger Games* (Scholastic, 2008)

me, but I used them as a motivator to push me on. My intention is to draw comparisons between you and me, for you to see that anything is possible regardless of age, gender, race or background. All you need is a good work ethic and a vision of exactly where you want to go. If I can do it, you most certainly can too, especially with me here fighting your corner. I'm going to hold your hand along the way, share my insights and give you my step-by-step guide to starting a wildly successful business from nothing with my Business Starter Method™.

Business Starter Method™

Like my diagram? It's pretty cool. I am a lot more talented with a PowerPoint presentation but I can't put any of my badass animations in a book (your move, Apple). Throughout this book, I'm going to walk you through every step of the process to creating your dream business. From the creation of your idea to marketing, getting your first client, building a personal brand as a young entrepreneur and even how to start your business with no start-up funds. It's going to be a fun journey.

The Steps To Success

Idea

You've most likely heard of the term 'million-dollar idea' – it's the most commonly used phrase in entrepreneurship. It's also called the 'lightbulb moment', when the switch is flicked and your life is changed in an instant – you've got it! However, we aren't all born with a great idea in us. It's about getting creative, becoming hyper-aware of problems that need to be solved and ultimately spotting a gap in a market or in an industry where you can offer a new brand. You're an entrepreneur; a problem solver. Your mission is to serve your ideal client, but who are they? We will dive into it all so that you can create the next million-dollar idea.

Brand

Branding goes beyond your logo design and brand colours (although we look at that too). Your brand is represented at every touch point with your audience, or anyone who interacts with your brand. It can be a handshake, an image of you on social media or a returning client. It is one of the most powerful tools that enabled me to build a seven-figure business by nineteen. I stood out; I wasn't like anyone or any brand in my industry. With this experience of building my home staging brand I'm going to draw parallels between staging homes and staging your brand. We will look at brand awareness offline and online from your brand pillars right down to your personal style as an entrepreneur.

Marketing

Marketing is the lifeblood of your business; without it, your business doesn't exist. In a world of overwhelming marketing advice and being bombarded with marketing ourselves every day, how do you decide the best way to market your new ideas? Having marketed both offline and online businesses, I'm going to share with you the traditional types of marketing that had the biggest impact in my career and the organic online marketing strategies that I used to scale to seven figures in the short space of three years.

Value

In a crowded marketplace, the most important tool in your arsenal is adding value. Throughout your online marketing content and the product or service you offer clients, you need to think: 'How am I adding value and transforming their lives?' The value you add to a consumer's life is becoming a valued currency that is in short supply; however, it's becoming an expectation from brands across the world. We look at identifying the transformation that your audience is looking for and also how to turn their pain points into pleasure points.

Growth

Once you have the basics of your business in motion, you're starting to implement the teachings of this book. You are profile seeding, building your brand, getting clients through the door and money in the bank. How do we go to our next level and grow? We look at growing your team, finding the right coach, productivity hacks and ultimately taking the next step in growing your brand. You've arrived at your destination and your next level awaits.

Mindset

Mindset encompasses everything in life and business. Why? Because it's going to be your biggest roadblock to getting where you want to go. Who knew? You might have thought it was going to be a lack of funds, or not knowing how to create Facebook ads, or coming up with your business idea in the first place. Nope. It's going to be yourself. Throughout our time together, I'm going to make you aware of the questions that may arise in your own head, the struggle you may be feeling internally to take a risk or a leap or to tell your friends and family what you are doing. It's not an easy path you have chosen, but my biggest wish for you reading this book is to remain mindful and stay aware of the voices in your head that are going to try to keep you in your comfort zone. You like being comfortable. Admit it. So do I, we all do. I'm resistant to trying new things, meeting new people, going into a situation that I've never been in before, and that's exactly what starting a business is. It's uncomfortable, it's uncertain. However, if you want to be an entrepreneur, you'd better get comfortable with being uncomfortable. It's the only place that you will ever thrive and grow.

Enjoy The Journey

I want to get it out of your mind right now: you can't win at this. You can't win at business, so technically you can't fail. One of my favourite sayings from one of my mentors Tony Robbins is: 'If you aren't growing, you are dying'.[3] Think of this long road as a growth experience. I'm a big goal setter – I will work my socks off until I reach the goal that I have in mind. That has created in me a 'what's next?' mentality. Every time I've reached a goal, smashed that glass ceiling, I experience a big dip in energy – why? I've forgot to enjoy the journey. I've been so excited about reaching the mountain top, I forgot to take stock and enjoy the scenery along the way. I have been hustling and struggling to reach the top, forgetting to stop and take a look at the view. I warn you now: when you reach your goals with the dream home, the dream car and everything else you want, which I know you are going to achieve, you are going to look back on the day you picked up this book and started with the first steps to building your business. I do it every day; I remember the first day I designed my logo and started to build my own little empire.

Decide On Your Vision

You've now got some idea of what you've signed up for in purchasing this book, and thank you, by the way, it means a lot. It has been on my vision board for a long time, and I'm so grateful that you have helped make

---

3   T Banta, 'Is Innovation for You?' Venture Greatly (blog post, 23 May 2017), https://venturegreatly.com/blog/is-innovation-for-you, accessed April 2020

this possible. Vision board – say what? Have you heard of one of those? Better yet, have you got one?

Oh, you are in for a treat. I've got a story for you regarding vision boards; they changed my life. When I was sixteen and had just started out in business, I had no goals written down, and my ultimate goal was to enjoy what I do and 'make money'. But the world is a funny place and it likes specifics, just as our audience and followers do. To put this in context, have you ever bought yourself a jacket or new shoes that you absolutely love? And you're wearing them, feeling flash, but all of a sudden you are out and realise that someone else is wearing them too, and another person. And another person. How dare they? I thought these were special. That's because you start to see what you focus on, and it's a little bit like that when you are growing your business. If you have a destination in mind, all of your energy is going to go there and you're more likely to achieve that goal than if you just wandered aimlessly. When I was sixteen, I had started to make a decent amount of income, around £1,000 per month. That sounds pretty good, doesn't it? However, I wasn't earning it consistently.

I had read about vision boards, and knew it was something I should be doing. A vision board is a collage of images and words representing a person's wishes or goals, intended to serve as inspiration or motivation. You can do it on your laptop, but I really prefer to get paper and glue and print out the images that inspire me. Thinking I was a cool teen (I really wasn't), I didn't need to do that, until one day I thought I'd give it a go. I got over myself and I still create vision boards today. I add different images of my dream home and life. With a giant piece of card, a glue stick (at least school taught me how to use one of those), some handwritten goals, two images of Louboutin shoes and two black female silhouettes in heels and power suits, I took a stab at what I thought I could achieve.

My Vision Board

Yearly Turnover Goals

- July 2017: £18,000
- July 2018: £30,000
- July 2019: £40,000

Personal Goals

- Purchase a property by December 2017

I remember looking at the page and the thoughts that ran around my head. 'Wow, I could be nineteen or twenty and earn £30,000 per year. That's amazing but I don't think I'll ever be able to achieve that. Buy a property when I'm eighteen…no chance.'

I had set goals that, at the time, seemed impossible. I had never consistently earned more than £1,000 per month and I wanted to up that to £1,500 per month starting right now – how was that even possible? But the first month after I created my vision board, I earned £1,500. The next month, I earned £1,600. The next month: £1,600. The next month: £1,700. *Every Single Month* I was doing it and bettering it. I bought my first property in April 2017, eight months ahead of schedule. How was this happening?

Was I working so much harder? No. Had I had a new idea or started a new business? No. I had a goal and all of my actions became aligned with what I wanted to achieve.

I'll give you an example of how goal setting and creating a vision board changed my life. I wanted to turn over £30,000 by 2018. In fact, we turned over £1 million in a twelve-month period. Yes, that's right, £1 million. Create a vision board.

A little bit of advice from a reformed vision board optimist. When you are setting your goals for your life and your business I want you to remember one thing: get out of your head! You might have a similar attitude to me when it concerns vision boards, but, as I've just proven to you, it's changed my life and I still look at mine every day. Forget what anyone thinks or says or your own inner critic – just dream. There are two elements to your vision board: there are goals and there is a vision for your life.

Selecting Your Goals

Your goals are specific targets you'd like to achieve within your business. These may be related to income, milestones or a certain number of clients. The key is being specific and adding a time limit, as I did on my first board. Now, I know that one of your thoughts right now is, 'Liv, I haven't even started yet, so I don't have a clue what kind of income or number of clients I'll have.' That's OK. This doesn't have to be perfect, look how much I underestimated what my company was capable of. This is why I like to use a traffic light system to measure goals.

Red (good): Achievable with work.

Orange (better): Stretching to achieve.

Green (best): Currently seems impossible.

When placing your goals onto your vision board, I like to put my better goal onto my board, with the understanding that my business could achieve more or less but I am still happy with it. If you are launching a brand-new product or service, I want you to create a figure or goal that you think would be achievable. However, it could dramatically change once you discover the interest in your product or service.

Visualising Your Dream

When creating your vision for your life, what your everyday will look like, this is where things can become fun. I like to call this the dream. Your dream car, home, everything. You can add timescales to this, too. For example, on my board I had to buy myself a Range Rover for my twenty-first birthday, and I picked up the car on that very day. I wanted to live between the UK and Marbella by April 2019, and I achieved it two years earlier than expected. Remember, anything is possible. Here are some suggestions for your vision board.

Lifestyle

- Where will you live?
- What will you wear?
- What will you drive?
- What does your day look like?
- What does your office look like?

Relationships

- Do you have a partner? What are they like?
- What is your relationship with your family like?
- Who are your friends?
- Who is in your inner circle?

Health

- How do you look?
- What are you eating?
- How is your energy?
- How do you feel?

Business

- What is your position within your business?
- Who works with you?
- Who are your clients?
- What are you offering?
- How do you feel when you are working?
- How has your business grown?

Growth

- Who are you as a person?
- Have you learned any new skills?
- Who have you trained with?
- How have you changed?
- What do you practise daily?

Ask Yourself Why

Before you dive into reading the rest of the book and as we work through the method together, I'd love to ask you to take some time to work out what you want by the end of this book. When setting goals and creating your vision, you are becoming more connected to your 'why'. Why are you doing this? Why are you starting a business? Your why will be the one thing throughout your journey that will stop you from giving up, it will be what keeps you going when you are certain you can't. Connecting with your why now will put your business on track for the future.

Your Scorecard

You'll never know how to get there unless you know where you currently are. That is why I've designed a scorecard for you to complete at www .TooBigForYourBootsBook.com/scorecard

It's a set of questions designed to score you on the areas of growth we discuss throughout this book. It gives you a customised report based on your answers. The results of the scorecard will give you a starting point, showing you areas that you are currently strong in and areas you need to focus your attention.

3
What Doesn't Kill You Makes You Stronger

I'm a transparent person and I committed to myself that if I was writing a book I would share my whole truth. I'm going to put it all on the line for you. I want you to understand exactly what was going through my head as I was building my business as a teenager. We've just discussed goal setting and creating your vision, but I want to share with you that, although I created goals and a vision of where I wanted to go, I was immediately re-directed off that path and into a dark place that could have destroyed me before I began.

In the spirit of living outside our comfort zones, I like to embody what I teach. I'm going to share with you every part of my story, start to finish. You're going to hear what was on my mind and what state of mind I was in. This chapter is aptly named, although I hate the saying, 'What doesn't kill you makes you stronger.' It's not true for everyone. Why, then, did I employ it as a title for one of my chapters? It has been true for me on several occasions.

Letting Go Of Shame

Being interviewed is a funny thing and I feel for celebrities. Their lives look glamorous, which they probably are, but they can be intruded on and exposed all the same. For me, there is an equal feeling of fun and fear when it comes to interviews. They can be a completely indulgent experience, reliving the good times and achievements, or they can strike a nerve inside you. They can bring up something you didn't expect. It's usually the thing you have put out of your mind for a long time and filed into the 'I've dealt with it' box. Yeah, I know about that.

I was being interviewed for a *Daily Mail* spread on my success and my publicist at the time warned me to be a little wary. Think of that meeting I had with my publicist like the most recent TV programme where a staffer sits down with the soon-to-be President in an attempt to pre-empt questions and discuss any skeletons in the closet before the press get hold of it. It wasn't quite as serious as that, but you get where I'm coming from. The press are looking to share my story but they will want some juicy details to hook the audience.

I will be fine, I thought. I'm great at interviews, I have nothing to hide. Until, naturally, my school life came up in conversation. I would normally meet this question with a semi-nonchalant answer about how it wasn't my favourite time, my eyes glazed over and never fully convincing. This time, I could no longer keep on the mask. Was it the calm tone and rapport I had built with the interviewer? Or was it just time for me to come clean? This was the moment for me to step out from the shadows and to share my real truth. I answered in the usual way, but I got caught. I didn't answer with enough force and conviction. The interviewer probed further.

'Wait, I'm not ready for this!' I thought. 'I haven't practised what I was going to say!' I took a breath, remembering some wise words that one of my mentors had shared with me: 'If there is one person I can help, inspire or empower with sharing my truth, then why not share it?'

My experiences of being bullied were both the most challenging and the worst days of my life. If you have been through the experience yourself or someone close to you has then you will understand how I felt. From the outside, those bullying me probably didn't realise the impact they had. I had constructed the perfect mask.

I pretended I didn't care what people thought of me, which in many senses is true. It's why I was bullied; I was unapologetically me and refused to change for those who thought I should be something different.

However, deep down, I did care. If we are honest with ourselves, we all like to be liked. It's just who we are as human beings. For a long time, admitting that to myself was a challenging thing to do but, armed with a little more life experience, I know it to be true. It feels a whole lot nicer to be liked than it does to be hated.

'You've spoken openly in the past about being bullied...' That is the beginning of a question I was asked in a recent interview. I told you they had a funny way of teasing your feelings out. I can be blunt at times; that question made me tense up and become a little defensive. It was no fault of the interviewer, she was just reading her lines. But, for me, these weren't lines I had learned. This was not only one of the most challenging times of my life, it is still one of the hardest things to talk about. Talking about something helps you heal, but even when I was writing this book I really struggled with how to bring it up. It isn't comfortable to discuss, and it's a far cry from the happy-go-lucky rose-tinted view of the world you often read about.

For a long time I felt shame when admitting I had been bullied. I was putting my hand up and admitting I was a victim. I felt there was something wrong with me and that made people treat me this way. Now I realise how untrue that is. I would like to rephrase the beginning of the interviewer's question: 'You've spoken *Unashamedly* in the past about being bullied...' I'm getting there, slowly taking the shackles of shame off, one interview at a time.

If you take one thing from this book, I want you to know that if you are being bullied or have been, whether you are in school or at a workplace, it has nothing to do with you. I understand it's a hard thing to believe. I'm going to share with you how I repositioned the subject in my head and began to believe it. I was an A-grade student and I was able to achieve academic success without really trying, which may sound like a big-headed thing for me to admit to you, but I can only be honest. What didn't come easy for me was fitting in. I embraced how different I was and the level of torment I got for it. I became more flamboyant and stepped more into my own skin every day. You could say this was self-acceptance but upon reflection it was me taking control and rejecting their invalidation of who I was.

Your Story Is Valid

The shame didn't end for me when I admitted I was bullied and why I was bullied. Even talking about it has felt to me like I am pulling out the victim card and saying 'poor me', when in reality I have had a great life in so many other ways. I was nothing like the classic Hollywood depiction of a geeky girl with round spectacles and little confidence. I was outspoken, confident and sporty. I categorised my story as invalid or not valued. One thing I've learned is that no reason for being bullied is more justified than another. In fact, *No Reason Is Justified At All.* No one is tallying points up on a scoreboard as to who has had the worst experience or who should receive the most empathy. Your story is valid.

I vividly remember some of the incidents that occurred, and, in the interests of transparency, each one was instigated by another girl. I have no issues with women and I'm a massive advocate for women supporting women. We have been oppressed as a gender since the beginning of time and, if anything, we should have each other's backs. There is so much power to be found in collaborating over competing with one another.

The main memories I have of those stomach-churning moments (and they still make me feel this way) are girls whispering and laughing across the classroom at me. I remember seeing nasty and abusive group messages where people discussed how much they hated me and how funny it would be to see me fail, as they befriended my close friends and turned them against me with lies. If verbal and mental abuse hadn't been enough, for a short period before I moved school it became more insidious and harder to hide from. They would boo and laugh if I had to do a presentation in class. I was 'accidentally' hit in the nose and shed blood in my gym class. Someone left a fake tarantula (I have arachnophobia) on my chair. The final straw came when a girl emptied my school bag out onto the floor in my English class as I left the room, and I returned to find all my personal items strewn around.

Those days were unbearable, and I know if you've been through the same it has evoked the exact same feelings in you. We all have our own version. I felt as though any sense of self-worth or confidence I had was slowly being chipped away one piece at a time. I had endured four full years and I eventually crumbled.

I've crumbled very few times in my life, and I value that fact highly. I show up if I've committed to something, even I don't want to. I perform when I'm not feeling at my best. I remain positive and continue to develop myself even if things aren't going perfectly to plan. On that day, however, I was done. There was no fight left in me. I decided I wouldn't be treated this way for another second, minute or day. I was done. Finito. No more. I had taken the first step in shedding an unbelievably heavy weight off my shoulders. I abandoned my classroom; I don't even remember anyone asking where I was going. School bag in tow, I pushed open the doors and walked home. As I arrived at my front porch, I ripped my mask off and walked inside.

Reaching Rock Bottom

I've built that moment up to be a monumental occasion, a scene out of a movie where the undervalued employee tells his boss he is quitting, or even when the guy kisses the girl in the pouring rain. In reality it was quite the opposite. I was fragile, I couldn't speak for hysterically crying. I was a kettle at boiling point. It was one of my lowest moments. The girl who emptied my bag out had tipped over my final domino. Ironically, she saved my life. I'm grateful I had people in my life who I could pour my heart out to. Had I bottled it up any longer, I would have expressed those feelings of worthlessness in a reckless manner and who knows where I would be right now? I would never want to give you the illusion that all of your worries disappear in that moment. Speaking out is the first step in a long road to saving your life.

Once you've hit rock bottom, you're faced with practical and psychological questions as to how you are going to heal. How do you move forward with school or work? How are you going to remove these individuals from your life? For me, it meant uprooting and moving school. You've heard of the block button on social media, but it exists in real life too, which I will delve into deeper with you in Chapter 13.

One of the questions I'm often asked revolves around whether I have restored my confidence after experiencing slow but deceitful destruction of myself. I have a wonderful life now, with only those in it who truly accept me and love me for both my good and my bad; the true me. The experience has taught me to protect myself much more. At the same time, I have a lot less resilience, tolerance and ability to cope when it comes to being bullied. How do you start to heal emotionally? I'm not a psychologist or a professional, so I can only speak from experience. My advice would be to educate yourself by reading books like this one. It is important to come from a place of understanding that this has nothing to do with you; it's someone else's issue. That will allow you to reframe the situation. Finally, understand that you are not alone on this journey. There are many others and there is comfort in knowing that. When life throws you more curve balls, which it undoubtedly will, you will be better equipped to deal with them as a result of what you went through. We are strong.

4
Explaining The Big Idea

It can be described as the 'lightbulb moment', an 'aha!' moment or the 'big idea'. Sometimes it can be as simple as finding inspiration from your own backside. It was for Sara Blakely, anyway, and Spanx is now a billion-dollar business. Sometimes you've got to think small to think big. The most successful businesses are born out of a place of pain or pleasure. It could be from frustration you or someone else has experienced – the clues are around us every day. The key is learning to identify them when they arise.

My Lightbulb Moment

I wasn't on the hunt for a business model when I stumbled upon the idea to start a home staging company.

My mum was involved in property investing and she was flipping one of her properties. Flipping is when you buy a property and re-sell it to make a profit. In this case she had renovated the property. It was a two-bedroom, two-bathroom apartment with an open plan living/dining/kitchen space, but it was difficult for potential buyers to imagine how to use it when it lay empty. Viewers just saw an enormous kitchen. The property was on the market (unfurnished) for three months. There were viewers, but everyone who came through the door couldn't imagine how to live in the property. The vast majority of people can't imagine how to furnish an empty space (which means there is a massive need for the service).

I had heard of the concept of staging but it wasn't common in the UK. Most people don't know what home staging is, so let me explain. Home staging is giving your property the 'show home look' with furniture, soft furnishings and styling it as a home. Essentially presenting a lifestyle.

I looked for a company in the area who could stage the property for us, but I couldn't find anyone who offered the service we required. As it happened, I had been dragged around home decor shops all my life (thanks, Mum) and, after a lifetime of moaning about it, I had developed an interest in it, constantly changing my own bedroom and photographing it on my flip-up Motorola. Resourceful to my core, I suggested that we buy some furniture and I stage the property.

What happened next? The property sold in three days, above the valuation price. Oh, and the person who bought the property bought all of the furniture too. He wanted a walk-in home; we even left him beers in the fridge. Talk about a full service. Ding, ding, ding! The business idea was sparked. With these results, I knew I could go on to help hundreds of other people just like my mum make more money from their properties.

Finding Your Big Idea

As Marc Randolph, co-founder of Netflix says, 'It takes thousands of bad ideas, to find one good one'.[4] The adopted term for a great idea is the infamous 'million-dollar business idea' and I managed to achieve that. I stumbled upon mine, which can sometimes happen, but generally it isn't that simple. Netflix is one of the world's most successful digital innovations and the world's leading streaming entertainment service, with 183 million paid memberships in over 190 countries.[5] Marc (and his co-founder Reed Hastings) didn't create Netflix out of thin air – he had spent thousands of hours coming up with business ideas, researching them and discovering they were unviable, as he notes in the Foreword to this book.

---

4   M Randolph, *That Will Never Work: The Birth Of Netflix And The Amazing Life Of An Idea* (Endeavour, 2019)

5   Netflix Investors, 'Company profile', Netflix (December 2020), https://ir.netflix.net/ir-overview/profile/default.aspx, accessed 1 December 2020

In business, I feel there are two different paths you can take: spotting a gap in the market and filling that gap with a completely original solution, or spotting a gap within an existing industry and filling that gap with a different outlook or spin.

The first step in the process to finding your 'big idea' is identifying a pain or pleasure point. It can be found in your everyday, pouring your next cup of tea or shopping at the local supermarket. The secret is becoming acutely aware of everything that happens around you. What frustrates you? What do you purchase that gives you joy? What have you bought or invested in that has taken away hassle or annoyance in your life? What has affected your friends' and family's lives? When you open your eyes, you will begin to see opportunities everywhere.

Is There A Gap In The Market?

How can being broke become the one thing that will change your life forever? Take Brian Chesky and Joe Gebbia, the founders of Airbnb, who couldn't afford to pay their rent in San Francisco and noticed a shortage of hotel rooms for a local event. They decided to rent out their three air mattresses for $80 each a night. After receiving positive feedback, they started thinking about how to act as middlemen, using other people's apartments to make money. Airbnb was born. They identified the pain point – lack of affordable accommodation – and plugged it with their solution.

Is There A Gap In The Industry?

Not all business ideas are original ideas; you may want to start a business in an industry that exists. Take Roy Raymond, founder of Victoria's Secret, who was embarrassed when purchasing lingerie for his wife at a department store. Lingerie shops and departments already existed but Roy identified what they were missing and how they could be improved upon, and revolutionised how consumers purchased lingerie forever. Victoria's Secret was founded by a man – rock on, dude. For you, this could look like owning a clothing store, your own make-up studio, starting your own joinery firm. The idea has existed for many years, but it doesn't mean that there are no possibilities to become a mover and shaker in the space, to come up with an original spin and to create a successful business in the process. I didn't come up with the idea of home staging, and I've never claimed to, but what I did do was identify a gap in my country, where this industry was in its infancy.

Or take Netflix again; they spotted a massive gap in the entertainment space – renting videos from your local video store and getting them delivered to your home. This evolved into delivering DVDs to homes and then went completely online as a streaming service. A business idea can also change over time.

Developing A Concept

Let's say we decided to build a home staging company in the US, where many other such companies exist. We would need to stand out and offer a service like no one else, with a completely unique spin. In the UK we added other services to our business and identified a gap within our competitors' products and services. We are the only home staging company within the UK that supplies original artwork, original soft furnishings and a completely unique look in every property. That's finding a gap in a market that has already been developed.

I don't see another competitor offering the service that I would like to offer as a negative – it can actually be a good sign that there is a market for the idea. Think about it: if all bright business brands didn't start because someone else offered it, we would only have one supermarket, one clothing store, one pharmacist and so on. My advice is not to look at the market and ask, 'Who offers it?' Instead, ask, 'What have they missed?' It's what they have *Not* seen that is the key to your business success. Glass half full, and all that.

When carrying out your competitor and gap analysis, create a spreadsheet listing your different competitors' names, current offerings and their pricing. This is taking a 'bird's eye view' and you should easily identify the missing gap within the industry. It could be a certain variation of the product, a new level of customer experience you'd like to offer, or an opportunity for a lower or higher priced offer that your competitor has missed. I'm convinced there is a gap in almost every market, and it is our job as entrepreneurs to spot it.

Going Back To The Drawing Board

Let's take this scenario. You've come up with a product but you discover it already exists and has been created by many brands. What do you do?

If you can't find the gap, or you don't want to take on large conglomerates, then don't. Trust me, if you don't have the belief you can do it on day one, it's not the business idea for you. Plus, it's admirable to admit this to yourself. I have a no-nonsense approach to business and I have full respect for someone on *Dragon's Den* who calls, 'I'm out.'[6] There should be much more merit for entrepreneurs who know when to quit and when to stick – I've been there a few times.

For example, I invested £10,000 into an online store to sell home accessories and cushions early in my business career. I knew there was a gap in the market, and I'll always believe there is space for many businesses like this. But I quickly realised – after designing the branding, developing the website, creating the payment portals, finding and delivering the product to a

---

6   *Dragon's Den* [UK TV series] (BBC Two, 2005–present)

distributor and spending several hundred pounds per month on a monthly retainer for a full year – that I am not a product girl. Yikes! Yes, I lost money. I had crates of cushion covers that I hadn't sold that were depreciating (which I eventually sold to my home staging business). I had to take a long hard look in the mirror, although it took me twelve months. This business was not for me; I had no time, energy and enthusiasm left to continue the business venture. So I quit. But what would I have lost in my other businesses if I had let this drain take over my focus? A lot more than I actually lost. It's OK to go back to the drawing board, it's never too late. You have to live your passion.

As much as you should be passionate about your business idea, one of the most fatal mistakes I see entrepreneurs making is that they fall in love with their product or service. Their business becomes their baby, and, if we are honest, everyone thinks their baby is the cutest that has ever been born. What most entrepreneurs don't consider is whether or not anyone actually wants to buy their metaphorical baby. The most crucial element that is often overlooked in any business is asking your audience what they want.

Finding Your Ideal Customer

The secret is understanding who you are serving and what they are looking for. When creating your 'dream client avatar' it isn't quite as simple as 'a twenty-six-year-old woman'. You want to break down who this person is, their circumstances and also what motivates them to purchase. We can separate it into demographics and psychographics. I suggest you begin looking at the demographics of your ideal client as follows:

- Gender

- Age

- Occupation

- Level of education

- Income

- Marital status

- Location

Once we understand the above, we can dive into the psychographics of your ideal client. We then understand what is going on in your ideal client's life both internally and externally. Consider looking at the following:

- Their daily routine

- Their needs

- Their passions

- Their aspirations

- Their spending habits

We use the ideal client avatar to understand what our client's motivation to purchase from us is. People only buy from you if they believe you are going to provide a transformation for them. If you apply the right transformation spiel to the perfect product idea, you are onto a winner.

Sell Them What They Want, Give Them What They Need

I want you to think about a product that you have purchased. Let's say, for example, you've bought a new car. You didn't purchase the car. Well, technically you did, but you never walked into a car dealership and told the sales person, 'I would like to buy an automobile with an airbag, air filtration system, anti-lock brake system, automatic safety features and automatic transmission.'

You wanted to purchase the car for what it would give you. The freedom to go where you want, when you want, the speed of travel, the personal space compared to travelling on public transport. You wanted to purchase the car for how you would feel when you drove it. The brand-new car smell when you first buy it, the feeling of luxury when you feel your heated seat, the look on your smug friend's face when you buy a better model than he has.

What you *Wanted* was the transformation and feeling. What you *Needed* was the automobile with the airbag, air filtration system, anti-lock brake system, automatic safety features and automatic transmission. When creating your idea, designing the product and ultimately presenting it to your focus group, consider even at the concept stage how you present and market your product. No one purchases on features; they purchase on the benefits your product and service will give them.

How To Find The Client

Once you understand the target audience for your product and service, you need to find them. People like people like themselves. We often create a solution to a problem that we ourselves are facing, so if you are your own target market you can pull on your own struggles and frustrations.

Identify where your dream client is and carry out a 'focus group'. Nowadays that term seems so arbitrary. I'm still haunted by the day my school sent me into my local shopping centre, where I had to approach members of the public and ask what they thought about my tuck shop business idea. The only thing I learned that day was some colourful language. Think of your dream client and consider where someone like this may be found. Asking a group of middle-aged men if they like the idea of a female sports clothing brand isn't the right demographic – they have no interest in the product and *They Aren't Your Ideal Client*. Asking a group of twenty- to thirty-year-old females whether they would connect with and buy from your brand is a completely different story.

Identify whether your ideal client is part of a 'tribe' or, in modern terms, part of a 'squad'. If your ideal client is a divorced mum, is it likely that groups of mums who have the same life experiences socialise? It is. The next question is: where do they socialise and how can you get in contact with them?

Social Media

This is probably the easiest way to connect with a group of your ideal clients. We can be connected with hundreds of thousands of people across the globe if we leverage social media in the right way. Consider which online social media groups your ideal client is part of and make it as easy as possible for them to give you feedback. This could be an online form that they fill out, with multiple choice questions, or it could be hosting a video call with a free giveaway for those who attend and offer you their feedback. Get creative with this and gather as much information as possible on the questions they have, their pain points and what type of language they use.

Book And Product Reviews

Researching what kind of language your dream client is using is going to be a key element in connecting with your audience and building 'know, like and trust' with them. Looking through product and book reviews of different things you think your client would purchase is the best way to document their terminology and tone of voice. Keep note of these products as they could be an ideal partnership or collaboration for you further down the line.

In-Person Events

I built my business to six figures in sales through creating relationships that I had formed at networking events. It is a great and easy way to meet your ideal client in person to get an idea of what they think. Consider creating a mini presentation or a prototype to present so they can fully see what you are offering.

Assessing The Demand

Once you've received the feedback, you will hopefully have collected constructive information on what your target audience liked and what they felt could be improved. Your initial investigation into building your product is going to be crucial throughout all stages of your business as you can refer back to your clients' pain points and their language. This can often be great for keeping your brand on track.

Finally, ask yourself: is there a statistical demand for your product or service? For example, I shared earlier that nine out of ten people cannot visualise how to live in an empty space, which is statistical proof that there is a need for home staging, and it is indeed something we use throughout our marketing strategy. Assessing if there is a need for your service is vital, not only for the success of your business idea, but also if you are looking for an angel investor to invest in your idea or to bring partners onboard. Consider the demand for your service (industry-wide and then you can look statistically at what is required within your industry. For example, you may discover that 75% of the companies in your industry offer a minimum fee of $5,000, but you see a window of opportunity to offer a lower-end product that is more affordable.

Thinking outside the box is absolutely crucial to your business's success, but what will hold most entrepreneurs back is never getting their idea off the ground. I'm not one to sit around and not take action, though, so get ready for action.

5
How To Get Started

If you're anything like me, you have absolutely no patience. How do I know that? Well, if you're reading a book on entrepreneurship and you are under thirty, that's unusual. There aren't many people like us out there. They say patience is a virtue, but my impatience is a virtue, too. It is one of the many ingredients in the mix that helped me build a £1-million brand when I was in my teens. I didn't have the time to wait until I was thirty to get started. Nothing and no one was going to hold me back.

Have you ever run a marathon? I haven't...well, not the traditional kind, anyway (the only time you would ever find me running is if they had a sale on at my favourite shoe shop). I want you to think of entrepreneurship like a marathon. In our previous chapter we were in training, we completed our pre-marathon preparation, and now we are at the starting line. We have got it all ahead of us, we wait to hear the gun sound and we are off. At this point we are feeling optimistic and excited. I trained for this for so long, I put in the hours and I completed the training. Then, bang! The marathon begins and we have the realisation that it all sounded great in theory and now we actually have to run. We weren't prepared for this, so we think way too much and question...should I even start? Maybe if I don't start then I can't fail. I have such a long journey ahead – do I even know how to start?

Snap yourself out of it; you are going to the starting line and I'm going to get you moving. What have we learned from our starting line analogy? Starting is the biggest challenge. We overthink it and our mind plays tricks on us, making us question ourselves: can I actually do this? Why?

Having worked with one-to-one coaching clients and successful entrepreneurs of all ages, I want you to know that absolutely everyone goes through this at one point in their journey and for some it can be a regular occurrence. However, I've found it's more regular for young entrepreneurs.

Impostor Syndrome

Impostor syndrome is a psychological pattern in which a person doubts their own accomplishments and has a persistent internalised fear of being exposed as a 'fraud'.

I never felt this until I went to my first networking event. I was sixteen and I looked sixteen. I entered a room full of suited and booted middle-aged men. A sea of black suits, beards and an overwhelming scent of competing aftershaves. It was testosterone city. I literally skipped into the event. I had long blonde curly hair, rosy cheeks and I wore the brightest outfit. I felt so threatened and I hid behind a big personality that was an attempt to conceal my age. I knew this was going to be a tough sell to these guys as I was there to tell property investors, who were numbers and profit driven, that cushions, lamps and accessories would make them more money.

As a young person in business, my age has been one of the biggest challenges (in my own mind) and unfortunately I wasn't able to see it as a positive until I turned eighteen. I would never admit that I saw my age as a barrier to success but I began to realise it was an issue when quoting for projects worth thousands. I questioned whether I was qualified to be charging such a high fee when I was only a teenager. Of course, I was more than qualified. I had staged properties successfully with great results, so why didn't I feel as qualified as someone ten years older than me? All of this doubt, and yet I have only ever been questioned directly once about my age in my career. I gradually became aware that no one else was putting these limits on me and I was sabotaging my own success. Age was *My* issue, not my clients'. I realised it was time to get over myself. Oh, and I cut my hair (you could too if you have long hair...it will make you look at least five years older).

I had a constant nervousness that I might 'get caught'. It's a weird sensation and hard to rationalise. If I was asked, I would lie and add a few years to my real age. The day that I got caught, I was introduced at a speaking event as a 'seventeen-year-old who is here to share her incredible journey'. Busted! But what happened took me completely by surprise. The energy shifted in the room in a positive way. I had countless audience members approach me with compliments; they told me how inspired they were listening to my story, having achieved so much by a young age. My perspective completely shifted and I began to own my age. Now, I can say with complete confidence I wouldn't have had as many opportunities in business and life had I not eventually been open and upfront about my age. It has been one of the biggest reasons for people to champion me. My advice as a result of this is to address your age before anyone else does. I'm going to share more on this with you later when we get deep into branding and sharing your story but I just wanted to give you this advice; don't let your age hold you back from starting.

Launching Your Business

We've tackled that first challenge that may arise internally – don't sweat it, I've been there. Let's get down to business: how the heck do we get started? What are the first steps to launching your own business? Well, it's similar to my experience of starting this book; it's challenging. I stared at a blank screen for hours before I typed the first words. It was messy and, trust me, the version that you are reading now certainly didn't look like this in the beginning. There were hundreds of errors, things that I could have phrased better and that's OK. If I had £1 for every mistake I've made in business, I'd have reached the seven-figure mark much quicker than I did.

Here's a little mistake, just to give you a laugh. When I was staging one of my first properties, I had absolutely no money and I wanted to save every penny I could, so I cut corners. I forgot to tell my 'man in a van' that he had two extra sofas to pick up from the property he was at. When we got to the destination and he had to make an extra trip, he told me this would cost an additional £40. I was so annoyed, as this would eat directly into my profit, that I told him I would pick it up myself. I got in my little wrecked Vauxhall Corsa to pick up two foldable sofas. I could only fit one in at a time and the property I was taking them to was a ninety-minute round trip. It took me three hours driving back and forth with the sofas, and one hour to lift them up the four flights of stairs. Oh, and the back of one of the sofas was stolen from the public hallway so I needed to replace the sofa, which cost £200. I made a loss of £160. I was exhausted and angry. Lesson learned: cutting corners costs you money.

The journey, literally and metaphorically, is not always glamorous. I did warn you. I have so many stories like this to share. I tried to save money because budgets were tight but in some instances it can actually cost you money trying to save it. On that note, let's talk finances.

The Money Issue

Buckle up for the unsexy part. Another challenge we face as young entrepreneurs (as if there weren't enough) is that funds are tight. You might have some money from savings or from a part-time job but it's not that easy to access cash, certainly not as easy as it is for someone who is older and has access to credit. Business funding isn't easy to access in your teens or early twenties if you haven't built up a credit history and they won't even look at you if your business model or idea isn't proven. We don't have lots of life experience and we are seen as 'high risk'. On a positive note, the sum of money we need to make is a lot lower than someone with a family, a mortgage and a heap of bills to pay.

You can in some instances start a business with no start-up funds. When I started my business I had no money – I hadn't even passed my driving test and my brother drove me to my appointments. If I can do it, you can too. We've just got to get *Creative*, which as you know is my jam.

When I started at sixteen, I made a pact with myself to make the business a success within the first year. I knew that if I wanted to do that, I would not only have to come up with a strategy that would enable me to grow the business, but I would also need to make the money first so that I could actually carry out the service. I didn't pick an easy business for my first venture. Furnishing a property is expensive. I had no portfolio of work to show clients and I was asking someone to pay upfront before the work was even carried out. I estimated that, if I could just get my first paid installation, I would have one property in my portfolio that I could leverage to secure more clients. Whenever looking for a solution to a problem, segment it into bitesize chunks. I looked at how I could get my first client, not my first 100 clients. When you break the problem into smaller chunks, it seems less overwhelming and easier to solve.

This is how I structured my first deal. I was paid £1,000 upfront to furnish a two-bedroom apartment and I estimated that, if I could furnish the property for under £1,000, anything that I didn't spend on materials would be profit. Now, I'm a resourceful gal and I *Love* a bargain, but even for me that was a challenge. I purchased items from home stores like IKEA and hit every charity shop within a ten-mile radius. I even took a few cushions and lamps from my own home (sorry, Mum). I rented the furniture to the client for four weeks, which meant the furniture was paid for in the initial fee, and I would still own it after that time and I could then move it to another property. Deal one: complete. I made no profit but that was fine, I had £1,000 worth of furniture for the next installation. With just one kit of furniture, I worked out that, in an ideal world, I could move the furniture thirteen times. Which meant I could make £13,000 in a twelve-month period; not too shabby for a £1,000 investment.

Ask yourself these questions:

- How much is the product/service I want to deliver?

- How much will it cost me to provide that product/service?

- If it doesn't cost me anything, could I consider payment upon completion or offer extended payment terms to the client?

- If I have expenses to pay, can I cover them in one upfront payment?

If you are launching with no investment, I don't want you to worry. You know me, I'm an optimist, I really do believe that anything is possible. When starting your business, there are so many cost-effective business plans that you could start. Starting a home staging business certainly wasn't the best example, but it worked.

Minimal Overheads

Trust me, once you run a company with large overheads every month, you dream of the days that your business was you and only you. Bigger doesn't always mean more profitable, it can often just mean more headaches. When you are forecasting business expenses you'll have to consider the necessary expenses only. Do you really need that piece of software that costs hundreds per month or can you settle for the free version for the time being?

One Person Upfront

When you've created a team around you that are better than you at a chosen role, it can be a game-changing element in your business. However, this type of team costs money and drains your cash. Consider if there is a business model you can follow that will require only your current skills and time while you begin. Remember when you first start that you are going to be wearing a lot of hats.

Getting Out Of Your Comfort Zone

You've worked out your finances but you now need to take the first step: getting started. You're procrastinating, aren't you? Go on, admit it. Frankly, procrastination is going to kill your business. Stop it. Yup, I said it. Not only is it going to kill the momentum that you will build but you'll start to hear your internal voice creeping up on you, just like at the start of the marathon. It will say: can I do this? We don't want that. You must try to avoid procrastinating and overthinking at all costs. I love a little Netflix and a duvet day as much as the next person and on many occasions I've proclaimed it as 'self-care'. Newsflash: you're going to have to sacrifice that self-love. You need to push yourself to get it done. Living outside your comfort zone is where it's at, baby.

If you don't identify as a procrastinator, then maybe you are a perfectionist. Heck, I'm both at times and you're going to hear me talking a lot throughout the book about letting go of perfectionism. Especially when you're in your launch phase, creating your business brand, name and your marketing content. Striving for perfection has in many ways made me but it's also nearly destroyed my business. How? Perfectionism is amazing. You do everything to the highest of standards, nothing is out of place. Sounds perfect, right? But it can be paralysing, especially when we are in the launch phase. It's not realistic in business and it's taken me four years to learn that. Let's sort this now and I'll give you an example of how this perfectionism can become dangerous in your business.

At many times throughout the last few years, I haven't accepted my team members' work until it was so perfect that it looked like it had been produced by me. As a business owner, this is a relatively impossible standard. No one does anything business-related as well as you will yourself. I would redo the task I had outsourced to them until it looked exactly how I wanted it. I was paying to outsource and to lighten my workload, but ultimately doubled it while I paid for the privilege. I realised that my obsession with perfection had reached new limits. Had I exhibited the same level of perfectionism at the beginning of my business, I would never have even started. I had to get over myself. Business is messy and things just need to get done.

The 80% Cooked Rule

I have created a rule within my companies that I encourage my team to hold me accountable to and that is the '80% cooked' rule. With my home staging business, I look back at some of the first installations that I ever staged and I cringe. However, it's what the market at the time demanded, my clients were happy with the service and it was in style. Could it have been higher quality? Yes. Could I have spent much more time working on the quality of the product or service rather than the marketing? Yes. But did it affect the overall growth of my business? No. Did it affect our reviews? No.

This is called creating the minimum viable product (MVP) or the 80% cooked rule. An MVP is a version of a product with just enough features to satisfy early customers and provide feedback for future product development.

I'll usually refer to the MVP when we talk about developing the first version of your product or service but it applies to many different elements of business. For me, it means taking action and releasing what you are working on when it's 80% cooked. It may not be in its most perfect form, but success favours those who take action and it really is true that 'if you're not fast, you're last'.

Where are you in the process of developing your idea? If you're confident in your idea and have completed the research, what is holding you back from creating your first MVP? No matter how many focus groups, questionnaires or market tests you have carried out, no entrepreneur ever knows how the real market will actually react to your creation, so why not test it? You'll learn what is right and what needs improvement. It could be the product itself, the purchasing process or the way the product is marketed. Spending your time in the creation phase is important, but we need to get some eyeballs on what you already have. Implement then improve.

If you implement the 80% cooked rule throughout everything you create as a business, not only will you see the results, but you'll create a brand that listens to its community, provides what they want and makes a profit. To paraphrase the great American football coach Vince Lombardi: perfection is not attainable, but if we chase perfection, we can catch excellence.[7]

7   G Wojciechowski, 'Lombardi turned Packers into winners', ESPN (3 February 2006), www.espn.com/espn/columns/story?columnist= wojciechowski_gene&id=2318158, accessed April 2020

6
Brand It Like A Boss

You've just had the ultimate crash course in launching your start-up. It's all about getting creative, but let's get serious now. Once you've got your first client (I'm talking marketing soon – patience, grasshopper) you're in business. You could say that you've made it official, but you aren't quite Facebook official yet, let's not go that far. We've still to decide on a brand name. I will see you in six months' time. You think I'm kidding? I've witnessed many entrepreneurs spend months deliberating over this exact thing. I was in a female mastermind group with a woman who took six months to decide on her business name. She finally chose the name I suggested to her on the first day we met. Don't be that person. I've got faith in you.

It's worth mentioning that you can change your business name – it is not set in stone. You know that perfectionism is something I have struggled with but, whether you're choosing your company name or product, the following will accelerate your success by years. It doesn't have to be perfect. Are you noticing this recurring theme yet?

The Beta Name

The beta name is along the lines of our 80% cooked rule. In non-business lingo, it means a test name. It's a great tool for us procrastinators or perfectionists to use, as it's not permanent and allows us to operate our company until we can come up with the most perfect brand name in the world (which might never happen, by the way). Don't just take my word for it regarding beta names, they do always say get a second opinion. In Marc Randolph's book *That Will Never Work* (yes, someone actually said that to the co-founder of Netflix), he writes that the very first name for Netflix was Kibble, yup, as in the dog food.[8] How is that for a serving of non-perfectionism? Marc details how he chose Kibble as a beta name because, when the time came, he wanted it to be so bad that he would change it before launch. When you finally reach the point of launch date, it can be challenging to take the time to create a new name,

---

8   M Randolph, *That Will Never Work: The Birth Of Netflix And The Amazing Life Of An Idea* (Endeavour, 2019)

so just choose the worst. It's definitely a strategy I am going to test on my next launch to enable me to get out of my own head.

It's almost the same story as when I started ThePropertyStagers. We course corrected. ThePropertyStagers was not our first brand name; we were originally called LIVinteriors. Why? Well, because my name is Liv and we were in the interior design space, sort of obvious, you'd think. I kept our original domain name (I'm slightly obsessed with domains, I own 172 the last time I checked) and I redirect all of that traffic to my current website.

Improving Your Brand Name

After my first year in business, I realised my initial business name was a bit misleading for people. Why? It was cool but it didn't accurately represent the service we offered. We were in the space of 'interior design' but there is a strong distinction between home staging and interior design. Staging is a lower-end service; you aren't as highly paid as an interior designer because the client has no influence over the design and the property is not usually their personal home. After twelve months in business, we realised that there was a misconception about the service we offered. It's OK to pivot with your brand – think of your original name as a beta test. We launched, we made sales but we got feedback and then we improved upon it. Mainly because of the lack of knowledge in the industry, we needed something that people would instantly recognise, relate to and understand what it is we actually do. We decided to change the business name to do 'what it says on the tin'.

I consider myself a brand name machine (maybe I should have launched an app for this). There isn't one brand I've launched that I've spent over sixty minutes considering what to call it. If I had deliberated for six months over the name, we would have lost a considerable amount of income and we wouldn't have been at the forefront of the industry, riding the wave.

I came up with the name ThePropertyStagers in fifteen minutes over coffee. You might love it, you might hate it, but it works and it's an internationally recognised brand in the industry. My motto: get yourself a coffee and just get it done. Remember, 80% cooked.

When choosing your brand name, here are some things to consider.

Do What It Says On The Tin

I hear you say, 'But I love brands like Apple and Amazon.' I do too, but at this stage in your journey, I recommend making your name as obvious as possible. Write out exactly what you do on a blank sheet of paper. For example:

- Property staging

- I am a property stager

- The property stagers

Voila!

Brainstorm Words

Any excuse for me to get my flip chart and some coloured markers and I'm there. Write down every single word that could be associated with your brand. Adjectives, verbs, nouns. No idea is silly. Start to jumble a few words together. I love to add ending words to different brand names, for instance:

- And co

- The X company

- Framework

- Method

- Accelerator

Easy To Spell And Pronounce

This creates brand continuity when a brand evangelist is raving about your product and it removes room for error. When my business was LIVinteriors it was commonly mistaken for 'Living Interiors' or 'Live In Interiors'.

Not Too Long

Ever been on the phone for twenty-five minutes trying to spell your website or email address? I know all about this, and it's even worse for me, I'm Scottish. Always think *As Easy As Possible*.

Get Feedback

I love to test brand names with my team, or, if you don't have one of those yet, just friends and family. They can be a great indicator if the name is catchy and cool or if you're losing your mind adding crazy words together.

Your Brand's Feel

Finished your coffee yet? Great, that means we've got your brand name, now let's get some feels. Yes, you heard me right, 'feels'. You may not realise it but everything in your life has been influenced by a brand, the brand that sold you the product. The chair you are sitting in, chosen by the restaurant you are in, the artist who is playing as you read this book. Everything you are engaging with is creating a feeling and an emotion for you. Deciding on the direction of your brand look and feel will completely change the experience for your audience and, most importantly, clients. How you design this will affect who interacts with your brand and why. One of my favourite strategies to discover what I would like to see for my business begins with looking at what I currently connect with as a consumer and why.

Brands You Love

Take Apple, the king of branding. Can you tell I'm a loyal fan? I talk about them often because I have great memories and experiences connected to them. When I purchase a product from Apple, it immediately strikes me as a luxurious product, which is important to me as a consumer. At every touch point, I feel important, held and looked after. If it's online there's a seamless website, immaculate branding and friendly online chat team members. When I walk into their stores I feel special as I've booked an appointment and they leave each other little notes on the system to say 'the girl in pink is Liv' and I'm greeted by name by my 'Apple Genius'. Isn't that genius? Once I get home after purchasing, they have put so much thought into just opening their boxes...it's perfectly timed to open in a specified number of seconds so that anticipation builds. Even the box itself is an experience. Just writing about it is inspiring me to purchase another product. Consider if there are any brands for you that evoke the same feelings. What brand could you not live without? That is the brand you want to embody.

Your Competitors

Once you've discovered what brands you have personally connected with, your next step is to look at
what others in your space are doing. Look at logo
design and the cohesive feel of their online profiles and
website. I would use this investigation as an adventure
of discovering what you like and also to spot if there
is a gap in the market. Whether you are designing a
new brand or a new product or service within your
business, researching the market is a crucial step in the
process before creation. Remember, you are looking to
differentiate yourself, so taking elements for inspiration is OK, but you want your brand to be completely
different. When I designed ThePropertyStagers brand
I took inspiration from brands worldwide, creating
a document for both companies in the industry and
those in other industries. Immediately you will be
able to see what you like and dislike about branding,
and most importantly you will notice most brands are
mediocre, apart from a small handful. You want to be
in that handful. Be the unicorn in a field of horses.

Your Dream Client

When considering designing a brand, most often we
are our own dream client, having experienced the same
transformation our client will receive, meaning we
will be a good barometer as to whether our branding

speaks to the dream client. However, if this isn't the case, consider the following regarding your ideal client:

- What is their budget?

- What brands do they already engage with and purchase from?

Your Brand's Logo

The easiest way to be inspired to design your logo is to do the research as suggested above. When I was designing the cover for this book I looked at every book at the top of the charts for 'entrepreneurship', but I also looked at 'female entrepreneur books' and 'young entrepreneur books' as I could be classed in both categories. I created a few A4 pages with screenshots of the covers and took inspiration from there.

Once you have spotted the gap you'd like to plug and you can see exactly where your brand will be positioned in the market, get creative. Create a Pinterest board and pin different images, colours, looks and other logos that inspire you. For example, if I'm looking to design a new luxury brand, I would search for 'luxury hotel brands'. This can be especially handy if you are hiring someone to create your branding for you; they will have a clear image of the type of colours, fonts and feels you are looking to create.

Brand Colours

Ask yourself these questions:

- If you were a colour, which would you be?

- What is your favourite colour?

- Is every other brand using the same colour as yours?

- If no, then you are onto a winner. If yes, let's look at variations.

My colour was teal. I was always wearing it and it became my signature. Teal alone wasn't impactful enough and I wanted it to stand out. I also love the feminine and youthful tones of hot pink. Combining the two colours was a winner and it has become our recognised brand. If you place it next to the other home staging brands on the market, you'd notice they are all gold, black and nude – our brand pops off the page. The secret is to differentiate.

Now that you've got your physical brand assets down (name, colours, fonts, logos), there are a few more things to get ironed out. Branding isn't just pretty aesthetics; your brand should have a message, an impact and a purpose that will inspire and motivate not only you, but your audience and your team. In our next chapter we dive into your brand story, which is the most crucial element of branding.

7
Your Brand Story

Would you get in your car without a destination to drive to? No, I didn't think so, so why would you start a business and a brand with no direction? I want you to think big. Scrap that, I want you to think international. I don't want you to start out by marketing your brand like it's some kind of 'side hustle', I want you to start as if you are going to be the next Oprah. When I started ThePropertyStagers, although we were small at the time I always kept the big picture in mind. As a result we are now in a position to license our brand across the nation; we have built a brand that is recognised, desirable and scalable. What do I mean when I say branding? It's logo design and colours, but your brand is so much more than that. How you position your brand now will be the biggest catalyst to your initial success. I want your mind to think beyond that. Branding is every interaction that you have with the world. I love this definition from Jeff Bezos of Amazon: 'Your brand is what people say about you when you're not in the room.'[9]

The fact that you are reading this book means you have bought into my brand and you are interacting with it right now. If you follow me on social media, if I've ever sent you an email, if you've ever seen an image of me, seen me on stage or visited my website, it's all branding and it's consistent. I've been building a really strong personal brand from day one, and I was in that car with the destination in mind...I just didn't have the GPS navigation on. It took me a little longer than it's going to take you but I'm going to give you the coordinates.

You may be feeling a bit shy about building a brand because you are putting yourself (and your accomplishments) out there. I often hear people saying, 'I don't want to show off.' I'm asking you to question that fear. Branding is marketing. When companies like Nike release their newest advert featuring Serena Williams with a new pair of sneakers on, insinuating that they are what makes her tennis great, is that 'showing off'? When you're enjoying your Saturday night TV and McDonald's are enticing you with their new Big Mac,

---

9   SuccessStory, 'Reputation Branding Quotes to Grow Up Your Ideas', https://successstory.com/inspiration/popular-branding-quotes, accessed 1 December 2020

telling you how amazing it is, is that 'showing off'? No, it's marketing. Why, when we show up online or in the media sharing our latest new service or product or posting a great customer testimonial, do we see this as self-promotion and not branding? I'm going to guide you through building the confidence to market your brand and product in a way that feels aligned with you and connects with your audience.

You can read lots of books on branding but what I'm going to share with you are specific strategies to build a strong personal brand as a young entrepreneur. Always take advice from those who have already walked the path you are about to. Before we start, can I just rant a little?

Have you ever heard that saying 'fake it 'til you make it'? I'm assuming you cringe just as I do at the sound of it. Let me reposition what this actually means. We need to take a slightly different route to those with decades of experience when building our brand. Trust me when I say you really don't need those decades to be good at this. What you do need is to learn how to be a good storyteller to create an instant connection with your audience. The one thing that will define the direction of your brand is the confidence we instil in our audience that regardless of age we are the 'real deal'. I'm going to reposition this phrase as 'face it 'til you make it'. Face who you are by sharing your journey and personality, until you have the experience to start relying on it. We're going to do that by building you the best personal brand anyone has ever seen.

In this chapter, we're looking at how you can tell your brand story, which is the most crucial element to building a successful business and connection with your audience. In my next chapter, I'll explain the different ways you can position your brand to build awareness and instant identity.

Personal Brand Vs. Company Brand

I don't want you to get caught up in the difference between building your personal brand and your company brand. Your biggest asset in your business is *You*. You *Are* your brand. I built a seven-figure home staging company and personal branding was the tool that got me there. When I was a solopreneur building ThePropertyStagers, there was no delineation between me and my business brand; we embodied each other.

In both my business and personal brand, throughout all of the marketing it was me in all videos, my voice, I was in all of the photographs and I shared my story. Here's the breakdown of the marketing between me and the brand.

ThePropertyStagers

- 80% home staging related content and our property transformations.

- 20% my lifestyle, my journey and me as an entrepreneur.

Liv Conlon

- 80% my lifestyle, my journey and me as an entrepreneur.

- 20% home staging related content and property transformations.

However, throughout all of the content, I added my personality. I was the person who delivered the content, therefore I was at the centre of the content. This is building your personal brand.

How do we build a wildly successful personal brand? Even if you ignore the rest of this chapter, there is one thing I want you to remember: document *Everything*.

Especially right now. For once, as young entrepreneurs, we have the upper hand. We haven't started yet, or we are in the early stages of building, meaning we have the power of content. This will build trust with your audience; they will want to work with you when they see your journey. I have photographs of when

I launched my first business at thirteen through to now – at every step of the journey I took photos and videos. Heck, I want you to take a photo of you reading this book right now and share it on your social media. I want you to understand that, here in this moment, you have the opportunity to document your complete business journey, which will become priceless to you in later years.

It may sound pointless right now, but in years to come when you are standing on stage, sharing your business journey, people are going to buy your story and how you've got to where you are today. This builds trust with your audience as you can back up what you are telling people: you've hustled. My favourite content is the image of when I was thirteen and I was standing at a market stall in a freezing storm selling those fake nails. This all builds brand authenticity and shapes your story.

Your Brand's Tone

You've made it to Chapter 7, so I'm assuming you are enjoying the content that I'm sharing and you are getting a feel for who I am. I will let you in on a little secret. When I got my mum to proofread the book, one of the things she mentioned that she loved was the style in which it was written. She said it was like me reading the book to her. Of course, it's been edited, but my tone of voice, my bad jokes and my sarcasm have made this book unique and different from other books on young entrepreneurship that you may have read. This is called your brand tone of voice.

'Well, Liv, that's quite obvious, absolutely everyone has a unique tone of voice.' That's true, but they do not verbalise it in the correct way throughout their brand. Let me give you an example. If you were to visit a five-star hotel in Mayfair, London, frequented by the royals, I might be greeted by the doorman with, 'Afternoon, madam.' If I were to visit a cool, hip five-star hotel in Shoreditch, London, they might say, 'Hey, how are you doing today?'

Your brand tone of voice is what will distinguish your brand from others. How you interact on social media is another way to show it. I often use words like 'lemme explain' or 'yup', as that's how I speak. I'll always remember when I picked up an international award in Las Vegas, and an American woman who had been following me on social media approached me with a southern drawl: 'As I live and breathe, I cannot believe it's you.' After several minutes of chatting, and her telling me how she too was Scottish (naturally), she mentioned I was the exact same in person as I was on social media, except that I was taller in reality (not sure that part was a compliment).

If I were to meet you in person, would I get the exact same experience as I do when I interact with your brand online? If I did, this would represent true brand authenticity, which is currently the highest paid branding technique you can achieve. When I started to share my story and tell people my age, my business success boomed and I received more opportunities than ever before. My transparency inspired many to work with me. People weren't buying what I was doing; they were buying *Why* I was doing it.

Storytelling

This is the biggest missed opportunity for many brands. We do not know anything about the people involved or their brand story. Why did they start their business? How did they grow it? Think of the most successful businesses in the world. Apple, for example. I'm almost certain that if I say the name Steve Wozniak you don't have the same connection as when I say the name Steve Jobs. Why? Because Steve Jobs built a personal brand – he was a visionary, a leader and, most of all, he shared his story. You want to become Steve. Having coached many successful entrepreneurs, I've seen it time and time again. If you lead with your story, you'll win. If you are unwilling to share your story with your audience, you'll miss out.

Personal branding is storytelling and it will bring your brand endless opportunities in winning business, securing PR, winning awards and scaling your business; all of which we now call 'thought leadership'. Where and whenever possible, share your journey. On all social media platforms there are opportunities for you to promote and showcase your story. On your 'about' section on your website, take the opportunity to share who you are and how you got there. It builds your 'know, like and trust' factor with your audience, which can either make or break your brand.

Get Specific

Your audience *Loves* specifics. You may have noticed that I have tried to be as accurate as possible with dates and figures because I know my readers want those juicy details, as I do when I interact with my favourite brands. It creates intimacy with your audience and they begin to feel like they know you personally. Who doesn't want to feel like a VIP, with behind-the-scenes access? It'll always be surreal for me when audience members approach me after speaking events and ask how I enjoyed my latest holiday with my mum. Side note: living up to your relationship and engaging offline is vital, too. You may not know them, but they feel like they know you.

Be Transparent

Being completely transparent with your audience will build the 'know, like and trust' factor. People who follow your brand want to connect with it for a long period of time and see high-value content, but, more than anything, they want to feel like you are talking straight with them. In a survey, 81% of consumers globally said that trusting a brand to do what is right is a deciding factor in a purchase decision.[10] It can be as simple as admitting a mistake you have made in your shipping process or sharing screenshots of your business back end. Transparency is a high-value currency in what can be a deceitful social media culture. Using transparency as a tool in your branding arsenal as a young entrepreneur is valuable. Addressing your age and acknowledging the journey will be a great way to build trust with your audience.

Pick Out The Hooks

Your brand story is most likely not a short story. As entrepreneurs, we are pretty crazy people (well, I know I am) and we often have big whys, which can result in a rather long story. Deciding on the highlights of your story is crucial to successfully sharing it. No one cares about the time when you were seven and you broke your arm unless it contributes to your overall journey. Start by writing out a timeline of your life, from your youth to now – this is the stage where you want to cover it all. This is called your brand bio, which should be a one- or

---

10 Marketing Charts, 'Brand Trust Is Becoming More Important: Here Are Some Key Stats And Themes' (10 July 2019), www.marketingcharts.com/brand-related/brand-loyalty-109127, accessed 17 November 2020

two-page document. Highlight any key moments in your story. These could be moments where you questioned if you could do it, key people of influence in your life, turning points or accomplishments. You are looking to have three to five highlighted points that ideally represent your start, middle and current position.

I will share mine with you as an example (note that I'm building brand transparency here):

- I was bullied at school.

- Everyone doubted that I could do it.

- I started my business at sixteen with no start-up funds.

- I built a £1-million brand by nineteen.

The Newspaper Headline Theory

Take each of your highlighted points and ask yourself: could this be a newspaper headline? I've included some of the real newspaper headlines I've had written about me through the years.

'The ANTI-Snowflake: Straight A student set up her first business at 13, left school at 16 and just a few years later runs a property company turning over £1 MILLION a year (but has

to work 18 hour days, seven days a week to achieve it).'
   – *Daily Mail*[11]

'Bullied schoolgirl to £1m businesswoman at 20.'
   – BBC[12]

'Bothwell teen left school at 16 and set up firm to deliver £1m turnover.'
   – *Daily Record*[13]

Your headline title often looks like 'From X to X'. If you are worried that you haven't yet achieved anything with your business, work with what you have; these headlines will change throughout your career and will become more exciting the more experience you gain. You can easily identify some of my hooks throughout the three headlines: bullied, my age, my business achievement.

11   C Driver, 'The ANTI-Snowflake' (MailOnline, 17 January 2019), www.dailymail.co.uk/femail/article-6599627/Millennial-20-runs -business-turning-1MILLION-year.html, accessed 17 November 2020
12   C Lyst, 'Bullied schoolgirl to £1m businesswoman at 20' (BBC News, 18 January 2019), www.bbc.co.uk/news/uk-scotland-glasgow-west -46921079, accessed 17 November 2020
13   R Mitchell, 'Bothwell teen left school at 16 and set up firm to deliver £1m turnover' (*Daily Record*, 23 July 2018), www.dailyrecord.co.uk /news/local-news/bothwell-teen-left-school-16-12952381, accessed 17 November 2020

Once you've got your brand story down, it will support you for the rest of your entrepreneurial career while also coming in handy for our next few chapters, as your brand story will be implemented in every element of your brand. Online, offline and throughout your content, your brand is every touchpoint with your client. Now that we know who you are as a brand, we can position you.

Not everyone who reads this book will take action. But if you are one of the very few who is ready, who is hungry for massive success and wants to become the go-to expert in your industry, then I have a special invitation especially for you. In my online bonus chapter, I share with you the secrets about becoming a thought leader and raising your profile.

Visit: www.TooBigForYourBootsBook.com/bonus

8
Position Your Brand

Are you tired of me talking about branding? Well, it ain't over yet, so stick with me. You are going to enjoy this chapter – we get to have a bit of fun designing who you are and what you want to be remembered for. I love the word 'design', especially when it comes to designing your life or business. It feels like we are taking power into our own hands. If you design something, it's usually to your personal taste and preference. Having built my home staging company from nothing aged sixteen, my education on branding was through taking action and I have learned so much via trial and error. I wasn't always aware of the strategies I was using until my brand started to gain traction and I realised I had a knack for branding.

Building a seven-figure business by nineteen was no easy feat and I attribute much of that success to the strategies I'm sharing with you throughout this book, in particular this chapter. Having designed my own brand, a unique message and an instantly recognisable profile, I have recently started to coach other entrepreneurs to do the same. I have gone from staging homes to staging brands. There are many direct correlations between staging a home and designing your brand.

Foundations

A good house is built on a solid foundation and is built from the ground up, just like we are doing with your brand. The foundations you lay first will determine the quality and also the stability of the house. If it's built on poor foundations, using cheaper materials, in years to come the house won't be safe and it will have no longevity. If the house is built on strong foundations, perhaps using more expensive materials and you spent more time on it, the house will be of a high quality and will stand the test of time. Similar to your brand – in the last two chapters we have been laying the foundations in order for you to build a successful business (getting clear on your brand story, which is the foundation that will help you decide your brand direction and purpose. It will influence all your marketing, new products and services).

Exterior

The exterior of the home is the first impression anyone has of a home, it's your 'kerb appeal'. Just like your first engagement with a potential new client; at first all they see is your logo, colours, look and cohesive feeds online or offline. This is the equivalent of your first handshake. In my experience it takes someone fifteen seconds to decide if they'd like to buy your home and I believe an even shorter period of time to decide if they're going to consider engaging with your brand. The most important aspect of your brand exterior is to differentiate yourself from other options on the 'market' so the buyer is willing to take a look inside, to view and get to know you.

Interior

Your potential client is now in the house, taking a look at how you do things, how everything is set up and how they are made to feel. Just like viewing a home for sale, the client will have an inkling if this is the house or brand for them or if it's a pass. We can influence the audience by using our brand tone of voice, making them feel valued online and offline, being transparent and by being specific with what we can offer them to convert them into a buyer.

Staging

Home staging is taking a space and presenting it in the best way possible. Working with what we have but fully leveraging everything that it has to offer and capitalising on those opportunities – similarly to how we position a brand. As young entrepreneurs, we don't have decades of experience or a large investment behind us, but what we do have we can use fully to our advantage to show ourselves in the best light possible. Fully defining and using our brand pillars, signatures and style to connect with our audience, and seal the deal of 'know, like and trust'. The staging is our final phase in building a brand, and it is often the 'staging' of a home that the buyer will fall in love with, the thing that will make them purchase.

Let's take a look at how we can begin to represent the different staging elements of our brand. I discussed in the last chapter the difference between your business brand and personal brand (with the 80/20 split of content throughout your social media and marketing), and I've spoken to you about the concept of brand story. You'd be forgiven for feeling a little overwhelmed or confused as to how to pack all of this information into one brand. I felt exactly the same when I started to implement some of these strategies.

'OK, Liv wants me to create a niche brand that speaks to my ideal client, with one clear message, but she's telling me to share content on my story, my business and everything else. What?'

Fear not, sweet child, you are not alone. This is a recurring concern for both my audience and coaching clients. They are unsure how to get across all the facets of their business and how they can impart their knowledge, wisdom and insights. Most entrepreneurs are multi-passionate. If you catch me on social media, my core message is about becoming a thought leader and building a personal brand, but I also encompass many other messages and run other businesses while being known for this specific niche. How do I do that?

My Brand Pillars

Although I shared with you my core message for my personal brand, you will catch me talking about my journey, home staging, marketing and branding, and even productivity hacks. I can do this because I'm clear on what my brand pillars are. What is a brand pillar? I like to think of my brand as an umbrella, and my brand 'Liv Conlon' is at the point of the umbrella. There are three sections to my umbrella that I discuss throughout my online profiles and marketing:

- My home staging company

- Supporting young entrepreneurs

- The Thought Leader Method™ [14]

---

14 This is the coaching Liv provides for entrepreneurs who want to grow their personal brand and become thought leaders in their space.

I can be found to be discussing these three subjects and, if you were to ask my audience to define my brand, they would answer with one of these pillars. Remember, your audience will take notice and resonate with one pillar more than others. I like to choose a maximum of three brand pillars as you don't want to confuse your audience, and I'm working from my Brand Identity Blueprint™, which looks at three elements:

- Your business
- Your purpose
- Your expertise

My Business

ThePropertyStagers.

Content: my journey, home staging business, business tips, design tips, online course.

My original business that I scaled to seven figures will always be one of my most identifiable pillars, particularly because I became a thought leader in that space on an international level. A large percentage of my following is from the industry, and they follow me to hear my home staging business tips, buy my courses or gain inspiration. Within my personal brand, it's an 80/20 split with this type of content. I encourage this audience to follow my business instead, although I do still share insights.

My Purpose

Supporting young entrepreneurs.

Content: my journey, speaking events, raising awareness, my book.

You'll notice that there are strong links between my own journey/brand story and my brand purpose. Relating your purpose to your own story is a powerful way to create clear connections for your audience to join the dots. It's something you clearly feel passionate about, having been through the same experience yourself, and it gives you another opportunity to connect with your audience on a deeper level. Whenever I'm working with a client, I advise them to have a deeper purpose; your goal is to create a three-dimensional brand.

My Expertise

The Thought Leader Method™.

Content: my journey, personal branding, marketing, business insights, behind the scenes, my podcast, life as an entrepreneur, coaching, online courses.

This is my method of coaching, and everything I am sharing in this book is based upon the method I take my coaching clients through. Here is where I introduce my expertise as a seven-figure business owner. Within your expertise pillar, you can start to share content that is relevant to your audience, sharing your business insights, experience, routine and mindset.

Discovering your three brand pillars is incredibly important to communicate the direction of your brand if you are just about to launch your business. This is extremely powerful to establish in the early days of your business. When I first started my business, I didn't implement and distinguish my brand pillars until a few years into the journey. Once I did, I built momentum and started to gain traction quickly. Take some time to work through the questions below to define your brand pillars. This exercise will give you clarity.

Your Brand Pillars

Business Pillar

- What is your current business or new business?

- How can you share insight from this business via a personal profile? For example: behind the scenes, tips on running a restaurant, etc.

Purpose Pillar

- Reviewing your brand story and hooks, are there any challenges you faced?

- Do you feel passionate about helping others?

Expertise Pillar

- Your expertise as a business owner is much larger than you think (especially after reading this book). What have you implemented from this book that you could start to share (for example, creating your new branding)?

- Think of five pieces of content you could share about launching your business. It could be anything from your morning routine to arranging meetings.

Gaining clarity on your brand pillars will support you in deciding on the direction of your brand and what you are seen as an expert in. However, you will often spot me on social media chatting about other things, totally unrelated to my pillars, that are a little bit more fun and playful. These are my brand signatures.

Brand Signatures

I like to think of your signatures as associations people draw between a certain object, activity or saying and you. This isn't as serious as a brand pillar or your core message but something more light-hearted. This is where we can start to have some fun, inject some personality and playfulness into your brand while also building a deeper relationship with your audience. Here are mine.

Waking Up At 4am

If you catch me on Instagram, you'll more than likely see or hear me talking about how I wake up at 4am every day. I work out, do a 10,000-step walk and have breakfast before most people wake up at 7am. Why do I share this? I embody what I teach about what it takes to become a seven-figure entrepreneur (consistency, hard work, discipline and deep work). This may seem irrelevant to you but your audience will *Love* this stuff. Most of the messages I receive on social media mention one of my signatures and, more often than not, it's my wake-up time. It's created a fascination with my following; they want to know more. People like to be connected to successful people and also those who push themselves in ways they can't imagine.

Margaritas

Where is my cocktail emoji? Having shared images of my margaritas from around the world, it accidentally became one of my brand signatures (that can happen often, too). I'm sent photos of margaritas daily from people I know and don't know. People look at margaritas and think 'Liv'. Is someone going to look at something on a menu and relate it to you?

My Mum, Ali

Many people feature their kids or their cute pet dog, but for me it's my mum. People love that we are so close and work and travel together. She is my role model, and these posts get ten times the engagement. Ali is a fan favourite.

Think of a brand signature as something that someone will look at and instantly think of you. What could someone take a photo of and tag you in on social media? Take the margaritas, for example. My brand has nothing to do with them, but people are reminded of me every time they look at a drinks menu and this is when you start to build true brand awareness. Having interviewed hundreds of thought leaders and successful entrepreneurs on my podcast, Too Big For Your Boots, I often carry out the brand signature test on those I'm interviewing. I ask a random question at the end of our interview that is unrelated to the intellectual conversation we have been having. For some of my guests, it's an easy one as they have clear brand signatures – they love potatoes or they are travel obsessed. For others it can be a little more challenging. Consider what you do daily, something that is endearing, think about what your friends would say about you? What would you love your question to be at the end of my podcast? Who knows, maybe you'll be a guest one day.

Style

Now we've got our brand pillars and signatures nailed down, let's talk style. Branding is at the heart of every touch point with your client. They may be exposed to your brand months or years before you speak to them on a sales call or they add your product to their cart. However, they have already started to form an opinion on you long before you've met them. How can we impact this opinion?

Injecting your own style into your brand will make it more distinguishable, and people like to know the real you. One of my most successful strategies (but is really just me being myself) is the way I express my brand through my choice of personal style. I told you about my hair style – it started as a strategy to look older and resulted in my recognisable look. I believe that I have stood out and been remembered as a young entrepreneur because I don't look like every young entrepreneur.

The first time I realised how impactful personal styling could be was when I won my first business award. It was a fancy affair hosted in one of London's most prestigious hotels, the Savoy. The dress code was ballgowns and glam, but I decided to take a different approach. With a bright green dress to just below my knees and an iridescent pink coat on top which was down to my ankles, I was called the girl in green. When my name was called for the 'Best Product' award, I strutted towards the stage with the audience looking on; it was definitely an outfit to remember. I was congratulated on winning the award but was equally congratulated on my choice of outfit. This was personal brand styling at its finest.

Remember, personal branding is about standing out. My look is bright and stylised. However, I have always dressed like this; it wasn't forced. If you look at my social media profile, it is usually an array of bright colours and stunning natural and beautiful seascapes or luxury interiors (a little nod to my brand pillars). Deciding on your brand style will be key to you standing out from the crowd, especially as the business world is a crowded marketplace. Consider the following:

- What is your current style?

- Is it in line with your brand? For example, if you are a fitness influencer, it is unlikely you will be posing in long dresses. Or could that be a new angle?

- Is it cohesive with your brand colours?

- How are you presenting your images?

Organising your brand photoshoot is key to the success of your brand style. It's totally free and a whole lot of fun if you bring along the right friend or business bestie to take the photos. You don't even need a fancy photographer – if you have a smartphone you are good to go. I personally use portrait mode on my iPhone.

- Block out four hours.

- Arrange two to five locations to take pictures (the beach, a fancy hotel, the gym).

- Take five to ten different outfits.

- Take images at all angles and all vibes (professional, chilled, fun, goofy).

In our next chapter, I will dive into creating high-value content. When it comes to style, I can categorically say that it has been a special tool in my marketing arsenal, one which entrepreneurs don't use fully to their advantage. Create a cohesive feed of lifestyle images that present you and give the audience a taste of your personality. Niching your style can be a powerful brand awareness tool. It's instantly recognisable when someone hops onto my profile and it stops the infamous scroll.

Bonus Content

Remember to visit www.TooBigForYourBootsBook .com/bonus for your secret bonus chapter, along with additional content and resources to support you on your brand journey.

9
Launch It Offline

We're ready for lift off! Can I use the rocket emoji in a book? You now have absolutely everything you need to launch your business. You have your MVP ready to go, you have your brand dialled in and we are now ready to launch... almost. The final ingredient to add to the mix is traction. We need eyes on your brand. Business can often be a numbers game, which means the more people you have in the top of your funnel, the higher chance you have of securing your first client.

I like to think of securing your first client as a key to unlock the door to many more. It gives us experience, it adds to our portfolio, we can gain great insight and feedback from them and, if we have served them well enough, a great testimonial of our service or product.

However, before we dive into how to secure that first client I would like to take a detour to a strategy that will strengthen our sales pitch and offer.

Beta Clients

A beta client is someone who represents an ideal client in your target market to whom you can offer your service or product for free or at a reduced rate. The benefit is that they can help further develop what your product or service looks like as they aren't a full paying client. They may be a friend, family member or colleague. You can be working with your beta client throughout the product and service development phases so that when you are ready to launch you have social proof and a strong belief that your offering actually works. Make sure your beta client will actually benefit from your product/service and give an authentic testimonial.

When approaching your beta client, clarify upfront what working together will look like and get their permission that, if you achieve results for them, they would be happy for you to share that with a wider audience (this is the key). In many cases, you'll find your first full paying client is a recommendation from your beta client as a thank you for the work you've done, plus they'll be raving about you. This is called a 'raving fan'. I've worked with many brands that have created their first six figures through the recommendations of beta clients alone.

Facing Rejection

As you know, I'm always real with you, and I want you to know that launching isn't easy, especially when you're introducing a product/service to a market under a new brand and with little experience in the field. It's all part of the game that you are going to get a lot of rejections. But don't worry, I've got you. I was the queen of rejection. I faced a lot of rejection in that first year. Looking on the bright side (are you prepared for this cheesy line?), every no is a step closer to a yes. Cliché, I know, but *So* true.

It's never an easy feeling when you are told no. It can feel like a rejection of you but it's not personal. I still get nos to this day and I'm positive I've still got hundreds more to receive. It's just a consequence of being an entrepreneur but, hey, the yes list is a lot longer. My very first no happened in business when I was running my little hustle at thirteen. I had been friendly with the owner of the local gift shop, and I excitedly explained my business idea and asked if she would be able to sell them in the store. She said she loved the idea but it wasn't in line with her brand or her clientele. In all honesty, I was really angry and deeply hurt. It felt like a personal rejection of me, and, looking back, I had complete impostor syndrome. With years behind me, I can look back at the situation with my business hat on and understand her decision but I still feel that sting.

I have found the most powerful motivation in life is rejection. Some of the most successful people in the world have been able to channel rejection into their work:[15]

- Oprah was told she wasn't fit for television and was fired from her job as a news anchor.

- Walt Disney was fired from a newspaper job for lack of ideas.

- Dr Seuss's first book was rejected by twenty-seven publishers.

- Steven Spielberg wasn't accepted to UCLA film school because of average grades.

- Steve Jobs was fired from Apple at the age of thirty.

It's OK to be rejected; it's how you bounce back from that experience that will define your success. Every setback I've had has been an opportunity to be grateful for and to learn from. Let's approach the launch of our business with no fear, as there is no such thing as failure.

---

15 R Feloni and A Lutz, '23 Incredibly Successful People Who Failed At First', BusinessInsider (7 March 2014), www.businessinsider.com /successful-people-who-failed-at-first-2014-3?r=US&IR=T, accessed April 2020

Offline Launch Strategy

I've hit you with the mindset required to rock your launch but what do you have to implement to secure that first client? I have found that the simplest way to find your first client is with an offline strategy; it's easier to build a connection and a reputation while your profile grows and you have started positioning your brand online. Depending on whether your business is local or if you offer an online service, I believe it's an easier option to go local to launch. The first twelve months I was in business, I found clients completely offline. I wouldn't recommend a completely offline strategy but it's the best place to start. Let's take a look at the methods you can use.

Local Networking Events

I found my first client through a local networking event. It wasn't the first event I attended – it was the nineteenth. Discovering where your dream clients 'hang' is going to be crucial to your networking success, although some trial and error learning is involved. I attended many networking events; some I decided to return to monthly and others I never visited again as they didn't have the right demographics.

I suggest searching for events online and contacting the organiser beforehand to let them know you'll be attending; this will put you on their radar and instantly elevate your profile when they greet you upon arrival. Showing up at the event can often be the most challenging part (I used to arrive thirty minutes early and pump myself up to go in).

You never know who you are talking to. Never underestimate the power of who you speak with. I interacted with many people who I had put in a little box of 'I will never get business from them' and I was right – they never directly hired me – but I came up in their conversations and they recommended my services to a friend.

This won't be an instant return on investment. It could be your first event or your fortieth event but keep consistent with attending. You can build lifelong business relationships with someone inside the room. I still receive business from people I met when I was sixteen.

Cultivating Relationships And Partnerships

People buy people. The most effective way to build your business offline is speaking to people. 'What? Liv, you want me to speak to people about what I do? I thought I could just hide behind a screen,' say most millennial entrepreneurs. In an online world of direct messages (DMs), instant messages, emails and texts, the somewhat antiquated strategy of human interaction is dying out. Whenever I hear this, I think about making deals on the golf course. We don't need to be quite as savvy as that, but treating your contact to a coffee or meeting them at their office always wins.

When I was launching ThePropertyStagers, my rule was to speak to twenty people each day about my brand. I would preferably speak to movers and shakers in my industry but, regardless of who they were, I would tell them what I was doing.

Write a list of brands and businesses in your field that would have an invested interest in promoting your services. For example, I help entrepreneurs build personal brands through getting them featured in the press, winning awards and creating thought leadership. What other companies share the same clientele? Website designers and SEO (search engine optimisation) specialists. One of the best SEO strategies for your company is to be featured in high-ranking publications; it provides strong backlinks to your website and positions you as an industry leader. An SEO company works with clients who need exactly what I offer to complement their service.

Relationships don't always have to be outside the box – they can be as obvious as the countless partnerships that I have created with estate agencies and photographers.

Affiliates And Referrals

Marketing your business can be a full-time position, so how do you market your business and run it at the same time? The most effective strategy is to leverage other people's time. Instead of employing a fancy marketing manager or outsourcing to an expensive contractor, why not pay for results? Affiliate marketing and referrals is the perfect way to motivate others to market your product or service for you, and has many benefits:

- You'll receive a higher output from your affiliate as they are being appropriately compensated for their help instead of an employee punching a clock.

- It's less risk for your business as you are only spending when they bring you a new client, which is technically a free marketing strategy.

- If your product is sold online, you can offer the affiliate a unique link or code when a new purchase is made.

- If your product is not online, create a clear strategy of communication with your affiliate. For example, are they going to put you in contact via email or pass you their lead's contact number?

- Clarity upfront is key to a successful affiliate. Consider offering a flat fee for recommending your services up to a certain value or you can also consider offering a percentage of the profit.

Host Your Own Events

If I hadn't started a home staging business, I would have started an event planning business, so naturally I incorporated both. Apart from the branded cupcakes and banners, hosting your own company events is an accelerated way to build your business and profile and also make some money. Hosting the right event with the right guests will be key to your success. Events can be time-consuming and draining to organise but come with great opportunity and, if planned right, can present a high ROI. Here are the main elements to consider:

- **Get creative with the name of your event**! You may have noticed that I love to do things differently. With an array of events and online invitations that drop into your social media notifications, it's important to catch the attention of your potential guests. My flagship event 'Breakfast with ThePropertyStagers' was a spin on *Breakfast At Tiffany's* – it was a massive hit.

- **Time and date.** You've guessed it, our breakfast event was a morning networking and informative session with a complimentary breakfast for everyone who attended. Spend time researching if there are any local events that may clash with your event. Yes, I've got the t-shirt for this one.

- **Location.** If you have a premium service or product, ensure you're choosing a premium venue. My personal favourite is a meeting room in a nice hotel, with parking. Remove all excuses for guests not to attend.

- **Catch their attention.** How do you capture your guests' attention and make it a memorable experience so you don't end up as just another event? Think big. At our event we presented for thirty minutes to the audience, with a live staging set. We brought in both a bedroom and living room set and staged the furniture to energetic music. Guests loved it.

- **Monetise your event.** Will it be free or should I charge? Firstly, calculate how much this is going to cost. A typical event like our breakfast event will cost around £1,000 to host, with no cost to attend, as we know if we have fifty people in the room, we only need one person to become a client to make that money back. The odds are good. The business we ultimately received from that one event alone was around £25,000.

- **It's a numbers game.** The turnout of guests for your event is a numbers game. For a complimentary event, I expect 50% of those registered to attend, and I only expect 50% of those I invite to even respond to the email. Which means for a fifty-person event I need to contact 200 people.

- **The key is in the planning.** For any event, whether it's online or offline, the secret to increasing your turnout rate is in setting up the right systems and processes to remind your guests that the event is happening. This could look like email reminders to attendees and increased social media posting around the event date.

Speaking At Events

If I'm attending an event, I'd rather be standing at the front of the room sharing my message to a wider audience than speaking to each person individually. However, you've got to start somewhere and build a profile to be invited to speak.

- **Attend events you'd like to speak at.** If you want to pitch yourself as a speaker for a high-profile event, it's a good idea to buy a ticket and attend as a delegate first. Not only will this give you the chance to get to know the event organiser in person (make sure you speak to them), but you'll also have a much better understanding of the audience and content, which will help you get your pitch right. If you want to speak on an international platform and don't have the budget to attend a live event, focus instead on building your authority, getting experience at local and industry events, and making enough money to attend the events you want to speak at.

- **Get speaking experience.** Speaking at local networking events can be a great way to get experience, as is joining a speaking organisation like Toastmasters. You might also want to look into TEDx. TEDx events are produced independently of TED conferences and each event invites speakers based on TED's format and rules. The application process is tough but giving a TEDx talk carries a lot of kudos and, as the event is recorded, they will provide you with a 'showreel' you can share with event organisers.

- **Build relationships with key event organisers.** Most event organisers I know say they won't hire anyone to speak at their event they don't already know. Get to know event organisers by following and engaging with them on social media – you don't need to know them personally, but you should be known to them. Another tip is to add 'public speaker' to your LinkedIn profile (along with your showreel, testimonials from organisers of events you've spoken at and/or pictures of you speaking) as many event organisers search there for speakers. Many event organisers have a blog, podcast or book – so you could start by pitching yourself as a guest on their podcast.

Going Above And Beyond

Michael LeBoeuf said, 'A satisfied customer is the best business strategy of all,' but I'd like to take it a step further and quote my favourite entrepreneur, Tony Robbins: 'Our goal in business is not to satisfy the client. Our goal is to delight them. Our goal is to blow them away. Our goal is to make them raving fans.'[16]

A raving fan is someone who is overwhelmed by the customer service they've received and can't stop telling everyone about it. How can we create brand evangelists when we don't have any clients yet? Is this a marketing technique? Let me share some of the things I've implemented:

- **Finding out something personal about someone.** The most cost-effective way to create a fan of your brand is by taking an interest in them. Learning about their life, being kind and just asking how they are. It doesn't cost your business anything to give someone a hello once in a while, whether they work with you or not.

- **Gifting.** If I've connected with someone, whether it's at an event or on a sales call, I'll send them a gift and a personalised note to show my appreciation. This is often a book that I think will help take them to the next level or it can be a bottle of wine. You and your brand will be remembered for going that little bit further.

---

16 Quotes heard by the author when attending a Tony Robbins Business Mastery event in Rotterdam, 2018, www.tonyrobbins.com/events /business-mastery

- **Sending a letter.** Ever wondered how to stand out from other brands? Go old school. One of the strategies I often use when securing PR for a client is sending a handwritten letter to an editor with their media pack instead of an email. Try something like this with a client to secure the chance to present your services.

10
Social Media

W e've talked offline, now let's flip that switch. We're going online, baby. My business experienced massive growth when we started to implement an online marketing strategy – specifically when we became active on social media. I was late to the party. We didn't start to capitalise on the power of social media until twelve months into the journey. I don't want the same for you. It makes me smile when I think about the opportunity we all have at our fingertips with a laptop, WiFi and a vision. There really has never been an easier time to launch your business and have an international audience at your fingertips. Are you ready to take over the world? I'm here with you every step of the way. While you are investing time offline building your brand, your social media profiles should be actively ticking away in the background. My motto is: if you are doing something, post it.

When I first bounced onto the world of social media, I thought it was a terrifying concept. Maybe you are feeling the same? I had to go on camera and 'show off' – that funny word again. But, as I started to see the effect it was having on our level of enquiries, people starting to know who we were and our bottom line, it was too exciting a platform to ignore.

If you are feeling daunted at the thought of going on social media, tell your audience how you're feeling. My most successful posts are always when I say what's on everyone else's minds: 'I'm terrified.' I really did do that once. I was showing our audience a home we had just staged and there was a mirror behind me that I hadn't noticed. I caught a glimpse of myself and I thought there was an intruder. I jumped out of my own skin and used some colourful language. It was a live video...no take backs, but our engagement was through the roof. You see, authenticity sells.

Choosing Your Platforms

Before we launch ourselves and our business onto the social scene, I want you to think like a consumer. You are consuming this book, you follow brands and people who inspire you on social media. I'm often confused when an entrepreneur will say to me, 'I don't know what content I should be creating.' Come on, you know what you like. Other humans aren't that different to us. Consider:

- Which top ten people do you enjoy following?

- How did you find them?

- What was it about their profiles that attracted you to follow them?

- Do you feel they relate to you in any way?

Let's observe how your dream client consumes content:

- What social media platforms are they using?

- What type of content are they engaging with?

- What podcasts are they listening to?

- What articles and blogs are they reading?

- What online and offline communities are they part of?

- What companies are they currently clients of?

I'm going to tell you straight: being active on social media and creating content can be time and energy consuming, and I have a team now to help me. Ensuring that your strategy and efforts are targeted and have a direct impact is key to keeping consistent and avoiding burnout, which can result in an online detox (been there). 'Jack of all trades, master of none' comes to mind, and it's one of the biggest mistakes I see entrepreneurs making. Trying to be active on all platforms will lead to spreading yourself too thin and you'll be mediocre across the board. You may have a particular preference for social media platforms that you use in a social capacity but do your dream clients use the same one?

All of your time spent on social media should be invested in the location where your dream client hangs out. Becoming the queen (or king) of your chosen platform will help you to build momentum, growing a targeted and engaged following. Plus, the great thing about focusing on one platform is that you can also post to other platforms with zero effort using a scheduling app. Let's take a look at the platforms.

Facebook

Facebook was the one platform that enabled me to scale my business to seven figures. I identified that my dream client was forty years old and spent the majority of their online time on Facebook groups, engaging with their tribe. As you know, I started my business with no funding and have taken no investment since day one, so mastering organic reach and cultivating relationships within those property communities was key.

Worldwide, there are over 2.7 billion monthly active users (as of 31 March 2020),[17] with 1.73 billion daily

---

17 www.statista.com, search term 'active Facebook users worldwide', accessed 24 November 2020

active users, so don't tell me you can't find your ideal client within Facebook. It has many advantages:

- **Community building:** the Facebook groups feature helps you to cultivate community, add value and support dream clients. You can create your own group or leverage others' audiences by adding value. Facebook allows you to be added to groups of targeted interests. Through educating members and engaging, you can quickly form relationships and be seen as the thought leader in your space.

- **Build relationships with your followers by interacting and engaging:** Facebook's conversational style allows you to build relationships with your audience, using comments and Facebook messenger, which has an 80% open rate (Hubspot) as opposed to the email open rate of 15–25%.[18]

- **Create a public profile and positioning:** having a strong Facebook presence can help build credibility and position you as a thought leader. You never know who is watching.

---

18 E Hudson and J Lee, 'Is Facebook Messenger the New Email? 3 Experiments to Find Out', Hubspot (blog post, originally published 29 June 2017, updated 25 September 2018), https://blog.hubspot.com /marketing/facebook-messenger-marketing-experiments, accessed 2 December 2020

Instagram

Instagram, the platform owned by Facebook, was originally for photographers and creatives to share their photography. It has grown into one of the most powerful marketing platforms worldwide with over 1 billion users, with a focus on a younger demographic. Here are some of the main pluses:

- **Look active on Instagram stories:** with over 400 million active Instagram story monthly users,[19] Instagram stories bring you closer to your audience by sharing the 'behind the scenes' of your life and business. Creating a close relationship, they encourage your audience to engage with you, tell you their opinion and get to know, like and trust you.

- **Profile build:** build a profile as an industry leader and connect internationally with others in your space.

- **Showcase your work:** initially designed to share the world's images, Instagram encourages you to create a cohesive feed and really show off the quality of your work.

---

19 Mediakix, 'How Many People Use Instagram Stories? [User Growth Charts]' (blog post, 18 January 2020), https://mediakix.com/blog /how-many-people-use-instagram-stories, accessed April 2020

- **Collaborate:** Instagram encourages you to collaborate with others. Consider Instagram takeovers or just featuring someone on your page.

LinkedIn

Looking to attract a professional or corporate client? LinkedIn currently has over 610 million members, 90 million of whom are senior-level influencers, while 63 million decision makers and 92% of Fortune 500 companies use the platform.[20] LinkedIn has incredible organic reach and quality connections. Harnessed in the right way, LinkedIn could be a game changer for you and your business, for these reasons:

- **Professional people:** it's a community of often highly paid professionals, who are highly engaged. The network has 303 million active monthly users, 40% of whom visit the site daily.[21]

- **High quality content:** LinkedIn favours high quality content where the user shares expertise and storytelling.

- **Specific searches:** LinkedIn allows you to specifically search for who you would like to be

---

20 99 Firms, 'LinkedIn Statistics' (blog post, 2020), https://99firms.com /blog/linkedin-statistics/#gref, accessed April 2020

21 99 Firms, 'LinkedIn Statistics' (blog post, 2020), https://99firms.com /blog/linkedin-statistics/#gref, accessed April 2020

connected with. You can use the search bar or buy LinkedIn Navigator.

Pinterest

Looking to attract a female audience between the ages of thirty and forty-nine? Pinterest is your best friend. Although the platform is becoming more popular with men, it is still a 70/30 split. Pinterest currently has 322 million monthly active users,[22] and has several advantages:

- **Share thought leadership:** one of the most powerful ways to create high-value content is blogging. Pinterest drives direct traffic to your blog for those who are interested in your industry. Could your client be one of those who contributes to 200 billion pins saved on Pinterest every year?[23]

- **High conversion rates:** 82% of weekly active users on Pinterest say they have bought products based on their brands' content on the platform (Pinterest, 2019). Becoming trusted on Pinterest is a must.

22 Y Lin, '10 Pinterest Statistics Every Marketer Should Know in 2020 [Infographic]', Oberlo (blog post, 27 August 2020), www.oberlo.co.uk/blog/pinterest-statistics, accessed April 2020
23 K Sehl, '28 Pinterest Statistics Marketers Should Know in 2020', Hootsuite (blog post, 2 March 2020), https://blog.hootsuite.com/pinterest-statistics-for-business, accessed April 2020

- **Drive traffic to other socials:** linking your Pinterest profile to other social media channels can drive a lot of traffic to your pages and build audience and community.

Twitter

Twitter is a social media platform for short, sharp posts, interacting with your community and commenting on current trends, markets and news.

There are 330 million monthly active users and 145 million daily active users on Twitter, and 63% of all Twitter users worldwide are between thirty-five and sixty-five.[24] It has many plus points, including:

- **Profile:** build profile and thought leadership by being active on Twitter, discussing trends, the market and other news.

- **Reach out to local celebrities and press:** Twitter is the best platform to catch breaking news stories and get in direct contact with celebrities and the press.

---

24 Y Lin, '10 Twitter Statistics Every Marketer Should Know in 2020 [Infographic]', Hootsuite (blog post, 30 May 2020), www.oberlo.co.uk/blog/twitter-statistics, accessed June 2020

Getting Set Up

You've chosen your platform, and now you need to get set up. I suggest you set up on all platforms and keep active. I like to think of your social media profile as your first handshake with the world. Before someone has even engaged or looked at your content they are met with your profile, your description, your image and overall look and feel. Your profile should position you as a thought leader, with third-party endorsement and professionalism shining through. As it is your first impression, you will be judged by this. If you have an existing social media profile, consider the following:

- How do you feel when you look at your profile?

- Do you sense a professional you would like to work with?

- Is your profile active or is it updated sporadically with images from nights out over the years?

- Within the first ten seconds, can I tell what you do?

- Is there anything highlighting your story?

That might have been a little bit of a reality check for you, but don't sweat, I've got you. Let's look at the elements that create a successful profile:

- **Profile image:** is your image a professional photo of *Only* you against a plain background? Or is it an amateur picture of you and a group of others?

- **Banner image:** think how you can incorporate third-party endorsement into your banner image. Do you have any images of you on stage in front of an audience or being interviewed/featured in anything noteworthy?

- **Short description:** can you tell immediately from your short description who you help and *How* you help them? Consider an 'I help' statement such as 'I help entrepreneurs build profitable personal brands'.

- **Links:** are you making it easy for those who have discovered you to research you? Have you linked to your website and other social media profiles? Is there a clear call to action?

OK, your profile is set up and it's looking incredible. I might not be your favourite person after what I'm going to tell you but I'm going to myth-bust here: you're on social media for the long game. Sorry to burst your bubble, but you ain't gonna be an overnight sensation, unless you have a hilarious idea for a viral video, but even that kind of hype dies after a little while. If you're in business, you're in it for the long haul.

Remember my marathon analogy from earlier. One of the downfalls of social media is the 'highlight reel theory'. The profile of your favourite entrepreneurs showcases the highlights of their life, but those with a million or more followers have been posting and hustling for years. Go and check it out – how long have they been active and how many posts have they created? Yup, they've been there for a while. Don't feel down, I know you're dedicated to being a success.

There are two elements crucial to your social media success: first, speaking to your ideal client and second, consistently posting high-value content. It's pointless having an audience if we don't speak to them and it's pointless creating content with no eyes on it – we aren't just doing this for fun. Think about who is online and who is watching. Well, my friend, you never know who's watching. Almost every time I receive a DM, it starts with, 'I've been watching you for the past eighteen months.' (Cue creepy stalker music and awkward silence.)

Jokes aside, these are the type of messages you want to receive. Why? This person is ready to buy from you. Having been in business for a while now, I've seen the social media space develop and change, and consumers are looking for more value than ever before – or rather they expect you to give them more free content than ever before. Consumers are getting pickier with who they buy from and times have changed regarding what we provide for them as entrepreneurs and leaders. If you do your own marketing you will probably have come across the marketing rule of 7. It was developed by movie studio executives in the 1930s who realised customers needed to see and hear about a film a certain number of times before they parted with their money at the cinema. The same theory still stands today: a customer will take an average of seven interactions with a brand before they will buy from them.[25] That's a lot, and we know that sometimes that cycle can range from a few days to a few years.

Audience

Let's dive into who exactly is part of our audience. What I love about online marketing is how targeted we can be when looking for a specific type of person. Have you ever been internet browsing (or filling your cart with all the things you can't afford, yup, I'm watching you) for a pair of shoes and, all of a sudden, there is an ad on your social media for the exact same shop, the exact same shoes but with a discount? I told you, we're being watched. For us as entrepreneurs, it's an incredibly exciting concept; if they can do it, we can do it. Understanding who is watching us is going to be the key to conversion. Here is my Social Media Spectator List™.

---

25   K Kruse, 'Rule of 7: How Social Media Crushes Old School Marketing' (29 March 2018), http://www.krusecontrolinc.com/rule -of-7-how-social-media-crushes-old-school-marketing, accessed 11 December 2020

The Serial Engager

Who?

This person interacts with all your content. They are the serial engager; they comment, like, share and DM. We need people like this as they boost our engagement rates which means algorithms will favour you. It might even be your mum or your aunt...mine are definitely my top social media supporters.

How To Engage

Keep friendly with this person; respond to their comments and message them back. You may find they never convert into a paying client, they are just in it for the ride.

The Cookie Monster

Who?

You might be able to guess...this one has a voracious appetite. They will not only consume your content, they will expect it. They're in for the long haul, they'll be hungry for more and more.

How To Engage

Replying and engaging with the cookie monster is a delicate balance as you need to manage expectations and boundaries. Beware not to give all your content away for free – giving short handy tips may suppress their appetite until next time. However, the cookie monster is a warm lead, so funnel them into purchasing your product as soon as possible.

The Silent Stalker

Who?

You will have hundreds of these people, you just won't know about them as they don't want you to know. They watch your posts and your videos but never actually engage or like anything that you do. What I love about a silent watcher is that one day they hit boiling point and these are our 'I've been watching you for months' people.

How To Engage

The silent stalker is often the most serious lead. They are calculated, they have been consuming content and have made a big leap in revealing themselves to you. It is important to respond to them when they are hot, making them feel safe in reaching out. The silent stalker is a hot lead, *Ready To Buy*.

The Partner

Who?

Your potential partner. No, not a love interest. This is someone with a similar audience size to you who may be looking to collaborate. It may be a free giveaway or a social media takeover. I'm a massive fan of collaboration over competition and this strategy embodies it. It will result in growth in your audience and influence, while providing more value for your own audience.

How To Engage

Being clear and upfront about the terms of your collaboration is important. Splitting profit, audience and sharing an email list are among your options. I love helping raise each other up, and creating a partnership that benefits you both can be a fun experience.

The Influencer

Who?

This is someone with a much larger audience than you on social media and they may have stumbled across you or been recommended by a friend. The influencer represents a massive opportunity for you to raise your profile and to position yourself in the same league.

How To Engage

Respecting the influencer's reach and communicating in a professional manner is important. If you commit to showing up for the influencer, do it – they likely won't offer you another opportunity.

You may identify yourself in one of the profiles above. I recognise myself in all of them but I can mainly relate to the silent stalker. I'm a calculated buyer who will watch a brand journey for months before purchasing. When I buy, I buy big, and I've purchased £25,000 coaching packages after sending 'I've been watching you' DMs. Understanding who is watching you will help you curate content and cultivate a community. However, when it comes to growing your social media presence I suggest taking a consistent but laid-back approach to your strategy. When you provide high-value content (we're diving into that in our next chapter), consistently show up and speak to your dream client, the success will come. Just not overnight. Is there such a thing as a patient young entrepreneur?

11
Content Marketing

Now you have an idea of who's watching, we need to figure out how we are going to encourage those 'How can I buy from you?' DMs to convert. Yes, the holy grail. Lucky for you, I've been writing high-value content for a little while, and it has converted into seven-figure sales. The world of social media is a minefield and as entrepreneurs we are now expected to provide high-value content for our audience in volume. Successful marketers are no longer those with the deepest pockets but those who show up consistently, fully, transparently and with their ideal client in mind at all times. It's great for us as young entrepreneurs as we don't have to compete – we just need to differentiate our branding and always ask ourselves: 'Am I showing up fully as myself today and giving the world everything I've got?' For you, that won't be an issue.

I remember reading a blog post on marketing when I first started in business. There was one statement that has been engrained into my mind ever since. 'Never be afraid to put your *Best* content out now for *Free*.' This is now publicly advised by most marketing gurus but I want to thank whoever wrote that random blog post back in 2014. Mainly for providing high-value content in the days when it wasn't as cool as it is now but also for influencing the way I will produce content for the rest of my career. It was challenging to get into the mindset of giving my most valued knowledge away for free (given I had worked so hard and spent a lot of money learning what I know). To create great high-value content you must change your mindset from coming from a place of fear and scarcity to a place of serving your audience.

I'm going to share with you the type of content that will support you in building a reputable profile as an entrepreneur and will convert your audience, purely through growing your 'know, like and trust'. I scaled my business from £30,000 to £1 million by the time I was nineteen without spending a penny on advertising. I cultivated a community, built brand awareness and respect as the authority in my industry. However, had I not followed a few ground rules when it came to content creation and building my business through social media, I wouldn't be where I am today.

It's Not Quantity, It's Quality

I'm going to myth-bust here. I hit seven figures when I had under 2,000 followers. It's not about millions of followers, it doesn't result in seven-figure returns. This is the case for many Instagram influencers. We look on with envy at times, and wistfully think 'I wish I had X amount of followers', but these people are also the ones who open up their own clothing lines and sell three t-shirts. Get out of your head that quantity equals success, because it's the quality of the relationship that you have built with your audience that matters, even if it's a smaller one. Our aim should be to attract ideal clients who want to work with us, buy our products and services and engage with our content. You can have a wildly successful business with under 1,000 followers.

Consistency Is Everything

The biggest comment I hear daily from entrepreneurs is: 'I don't get any business from social media.' Well, how often are you on social media? In my opinion, consistent activity means daily. You want to be at the forefront of your audience's mind. I hear you, it's already an overwhelmingly crowded place to be and it's growing every day with new people, businesses and brands joining. The result for us is both a blessing and a curse. It is a bigger opportunity for us, as more of our dream clients are joining every day, but it's becoming an even bigger race to be seen. The algorithm favours those who are actively engaging. You aren't going to be seen if you are only showing up on social media once a month. Heck, I was that person. I used to change my profile picture once each year so there is hope for you. You know I love putting a process in place to keep me on target and this is what I've found to be successful in keeping me on track with consistently showing up:

- **Content blocking:** set aside half a day per week. I love to do this on a Sunday morning when I'm well-rested and I don't have the added time pressure of a Monday. Map out your strategy for the next week, create the content and schedule.

- **Scheduling apps:** I don't always have the best memory, especially when it comes to posting at the right time. Using a scheduling app comes in handy as you decide the exact time and date. I will also mix this up with an alarm a couple of times per day to remind me to jump onto my profile to check in on Instagram stories.

- **Content diary:** I love to write a social media caption when inspiration strikes so I have a daily content diary in which I write my ideas as soon as I have them. This could be on your phone or in a notebook.

Act In Inspiration To Avoid Procrastination

I know there are some days you just can't face showing up on social media and I have those days too. When I'm working from home on a no make-up day, and the only person I've spoken to all day is Siri, I still show up or my content schedule does. I've hacked it, guys. Make sure to prepare your content in advance – this can be videos too – to ensure you are consistently showing up.

Niche Down

If you've already been active on social media, I invite you to look objectively at your current content. Could someone identify your brand pillars? Your brand signatures? Who your content is targeted towards? If the answer is no, ask yourself who is it you want to speak to. Remember: if you speak to everyone, you speak to no one. What are your ideal client's needs? What content do they already consume? If you aren't sure of what this looks like, find similar people in your niche and study what content they post that is successful. Use your brand pillars and signatures if you are feeling stuck for content. However, with my content menu, this is going to be a breeze.

Create Thought-provoking And Valuable Content

Want to be seen as the industry leader in your space? Start acting like it. Provide valuable content featuring your expertise and opinion and it will instantly position you. Do not be afraid to offer an opinion that may be polarising to some of your existing audience. You could deliver this content in long-form posts or videos. I'm going to say it again: differentiate yourself. By providing a unique angle on a subject, your audience will be more compelled to tune into what your perspective is. If your opinions are that unique, you will create an element of FOMO (fear of missing out) and your audience will regularly check in with you to hear your point of view – this becomes powerful.

Think Aspirational

People like to follow successful people. Don't be afraid to share elements of your life that demonstrate your success, both in your personal and professional life. This could be anything from sharing the features you have received in the press, prestigious events you are attending, awards or what you choose to do in your personal life that others would aspire to. This is especially important if you are selling a course, programme or coaching where people are buying into a new lifestyle.

Share With Purpose

You never want to share with your audience just for the sake of sharing. I run every piece of content I create through the EEE method. Think of it as your 'keep' or 'trash' system:

- **Does it educate?** Are you providing insightful teachings to your audience about your area of expertise? The secret is to educate without preaching – this could be a piece of content mentioning the question you get asked most often in the DMs. This proves to your audience that you are listening and answering their questions.

- **Does it entertain?** Your post might have no other objective than to make your audience laugh – it could be a meme or something funny that has happened to you that day. I try not to take myself too seriously and add a little bit of humour and fun into my posting strategy every week.

- **Does it empower?** Step aside showing off, we're posting to empower and inspire our audience. I love to create empowering social media content through sharing a piece of my journey or it can be as simple as a motivational quote.

Types Of Content

I was someone who struggled to create consistent content in line with my brand pillars 365 days per year, while managing deliveries of furniture all over the country on my own. I decided I needed to create a formula. A step-by-step guide to the genres of social media posts that I could create time and time again. Social media is a powerful tool but when you are launching your business you are wearing all of the hats; you don't have hours each day to spend in content mode. Our content creation has become a constant cycle, I've got it down to a tee, and I can plan a week of content for my team to implement in two hours. I'm sharing with you the exact content formula that I coach my The Thought Leader (TTL) coaching clients through.

Connection Content

Your audience wants to connect with you on a deeper and more personal level than ever before. It's no longer OK to only show them your professional side. Creating 'connection content' shows your audience your softer side, it strengthens your 'know, like, trust' but also builds familiarity with you as a human being rather than a brand. Sharing elements of your personal life could be your daily routine, lifestyle, introducing your dog, family or partner, or a hobby or sport you partake in.

This type of content is similar to your brand signatures and is effective in your stories and your feed. It creates the sense that you are more of a friend than a figure, making you more approachable, relatable and likeable. When you are all of those things you'll convert a much larger percentage of your audience. However, this type of content doesn't always need a 'purpose' – it can be light-hearted, funny or random. We are building a relationship, not selling to our audience.

What this content could look like:

- A selfie of you and your family (in my case, my mum).

- A photo or video of something funny your pet has done.

- A meme that is highly relatable to your brand signature or ideal client.

- Holiday photos.

Behind-the-scenes Content

As it says on the tin, you are going to share behind the scenes of your business. Consider what makes you successful. Share with your audience what is and isn't working in your routine, business, team, sales, speeches, research and so on. The key here is to mix up your lessons with your triumphs. I like to think of this type of content as myth busting, being completely transparent and giving your audience a real-life insight into what it takes to be able to do what you do. Not only will you build that trust with your audience but, if positioned correctly, they will see you as the expert in your space as you are performing and creating at a level and on a subject they may not possess much knowledge of. The content may not be sexy or glamorous but you will start to build intrigue around your practices, business and brand. Always remember to share *What* you are doing, not *How* to do it, as you still need to be valued enough for someone to pay for your knowledge and experience.

What this content looks like:

- An image of you on-site if you have a physical business.

- An image of your desk and your whiteboard with your goals (be discreet, don't share sensitive information).

- Snippets from your weekend away to detox from business (showing both routine and lifestyle).

Ideal Client Content

Our aforementioned forms of content will build our brand and create a relationship with our audience but it won't necessarily be the catalyst for them to contact us and convert into an ideal client. However, ideal client content will. This is where we are going to use our research on our ideal client's biggest pain points and common objections and use their language to convert them. Do you remember I suggested looking at book reviews and Facebook groups to understand our ideal client's language? This is when we start to use it to convert.

You have no doubt seen a piece of content or listened to a video and thought, 'Wow, this person is inside my head!' That is what we are going to create here. Approaching the pain point can be a touchy subject and we don't want to alienate our audience and make them feel weird or ashamed. We must normalise their worries and their concerns and then back it up with the proof that you have already alleviated this pain point for someone else. The most effective way to show you how to create this type of content is by giving you an example:

1. **Identify the pain point in your first line, using this as a hook to read more:**

   Have you realised as you obsess over audience growth that your income isn't increasing, but your stress levels are? Has all the fun been sucked out of social media?

2. **Normalise their issue and worries and also relate to them:**

   Yup, ME TOO!

3. **Offer proof that it's possible to overcome this, plus first-hand experience of this issue:**

   I built a seven-figure home staging business through organic social media:

   - I had no marketing training.

   - I posted content I liked and connected with.

   - I was completely myself.

   - I didn't care about likes or engagement.

   - I had so much fun.

4. **Use self-deprecation, which creates likability and transparency with your audience:**

   I had absolutely no education on how to monetise my brand online. I'm telling you, my worst subject in school was anything tech related, I was the creative, art, music and drama type.

5. **Build relatability – show that it's possible as you were once in the same position:**

   But I identified early on that if I wanted to build my brand and become an industry name, I'd have to get on social. I didn't know anything about it. All I knew was...

6. **Offer education points positioning you as an expert in your space. Each point is relatable to what your ideal client feels:**

My target market: my business was born out of my own frustration, so, when I started, I was my own dream client. I wrote down everything that I would have loved to have known and created that type of content.

Myself: at first, I was terrified of putting my voice, my face and my words out there for the world to see. We soon hit our first six-figure month when I realised I should just be me – giggly, sarcastic, at times ditsy, professional and different.

Fun: people are attracted to the brightest, most vibrant person in the room and the one who looks like they are having the most fun. I had to be enjoying myself – if I wasn't, then no one else would, and who wants to work with a boring, dull brand?

7. **Again, tell your audience how this is possible for them:**

You don't have to be a tech genius, a social media expert or a certain age to be 'successful' with social media.

My marketing budget per year for a seven-figure brand is ZERO.

I built a seven-figure brand harnessing the power of organic social media marketing.

Pair it with strong branding and visibility in the media, and the possibilities are endless!

8. **Finish with a clear call to action:**

   I'm hosting a FREE ninety-minute online training session, which is going to show you the exact steps I took to build a seven-figure brand with zero marketing budget. The link is in the bio. I can't wait to see you there!

As you can see from the example, content creation can become easy when following a proven formula. Be careful that you don't over-schedule ideal client content – once per week should be enough.

Key Factors

When scheduling your content, keep the following in mind.

Variety

Mixing up the different content types I have just shared is vital to the success of your content strategy. You don't want to overwhelm your audience with the same content every day, otherwise they will stop engaging with your brand. I like to stick with an 80/20 split – 80% of my content is dedicated to purely building a relationship with my ideal client (connection and behind-the-scenes content), with 20% aiming to convert my audience and call them to work with me if it feels aligned for them.

Call To Action

While following an 80/20 split of content to build trust and content to sell, it is still important to convert your audience into leads, especially if they are solely following you on social media. You want to get your audience's email addresses. Calling your audience to be connected with you on other platforms is most effective when you are adding value. This could be giving them an educational PDF booklet on your area of expertise in exchange for their email address. Be aware of how you word your call to action. It can often sound demanding telling someone exactly what to do throughout your marketing, but as humans we actually like being told exactly what to do and what button to press. Don't leave your call to action ambiguous; make it clear and precise what the next steps are.

Measure

My final tip on content is to track your success with it. There will be pieces of content that resonate with your audience more than others, and unfortunately I can't advise you on which ones will, but you can. Tracking what posts received the most views, engagement and conversions will give you a clear idea of what your ideal client wants. If there isn't much between each piece of content you create, then just ask them what they want.

Creating content for your audience can often be a headache if you aren't clear on what you want to say and don't know how to speak to your audience, but I'm sure this won't be you. Strike when feeling inspired and if, after following my formulas for successful content that converts, you are feeling a little lost, always ask your audience what they want. Remember, it's all about adding high value for them.

12

Solopreneurship Productivity

'Solopreneurship' isn't an easy journey. A solopreneur is almost the same as an entrepreneur, with the difference being you haven't built your team yet and are building your business alone (for the time being). It can be a lonely journey as it's really only you invested in your business at this stage. It doesn't have to be but we'll touch on that in the next chapter. When I started out as a solopreneur I felt there weren't enough hours in the day. At times I still feel this way.

When you first start building your business there are so many different hats that you need to wear. You are the creator, the marketer, the customer service desk, the admin, the banker and the salesperson. The question is: how do you get it all done without sacrificing each area and how do you ever grow out of the solo life to employing people who will be just as invested in executing your vision as you?

Side note: you'll never employ someone with the same commitment and love of your business as you do. It's your baby and, unless they are joining you as a co-founder, a partner or a shareholder, rarely will they see it in the same way. In most cases it will be just a job to them.

In the meantime, we must get your business to a place where you have the capacity and the finances to bring another superstar into the fold. I should warn you that (although it's not the sexiest subject) I am obsessed with organisation and productivity hacks so I'm going to make this chapter as fun as possible.

Develop Discipline

Being your own boss seems like the coolest job in the world but the reality can look slightly different. You may be able to decide your own hours, roll out of bed and start work at noon but I've discovered that the main trait you need to be a successful entrepreneur is discipline. Not the most playful quality but, without discipline, you're quickly going to be handed a one-way ticket to nine-to-five reality. Holding yourself accountable and keeping on track can result in a lack of motivation, mainly caused by lack of routine. If you ask me, productivity is the best drug around, hence why I wake up at 4am to seize the best hours of the day (I did warn you I am a weirdo). If discipline and routine are something you struggle to keep up without an accountability partner, I suggest you start as you mean to go on. From your first day you need to create a routine and follow it, even at the weekends, allowing yourself a cheeky duvet day on the sofa only once in a while.

Discovering how you work best is going to be key to your success. I'm a morning person – it's one of my brand signatures. You might be a night owl. I don't get you, I'm useless after 6pm. Given we are so in sync, however, I have a feeling you may be a morning person too. Learning from those more successful than myself, I studied some of the most successful entrepreneurs' daily routines and modelled my own on theirs. And I noticed there was one main message: 'If you win the morning, you win the day'.

As Tim Ferriss, international best-selling author of *The 4-Hour Work Week* (one of my favourite books – it will change the way you work) says: 'How you start your day off is vital to your day, and quality of life',[26] When I start my morning right, I build momentum for the rest of the day. Based upon Tony Robbins' 'hour of

---

26   T Ferriss, *The 4-Hour Work Week* (Vermilion, 2011)

power',[27] I make sure that before starting my work I take time to myself to learn, grow, reflect and move. It looks a little like this:

- Writing in a gratitude journal or expressing gratitude outwardly.

- Journaling goals and future plans.

- Exercising, stretching or going for a brisk walk.

- Watching or reading something inspirational or uplifting.

- Having a healthy breakfast and preparing a healthy lunch.

A Glimpse Of My Schedule

4am: Wake Up And Thirty Minutes Of Personal Development

This looks different for me each morning. I may be reading my current book, listening to a podcast or taking part in thirty minutes of studying. Dedicating the first section of your day to developing your mind sets your mind up for the day ahead. It reminds you internally that every day you should be improving.

---

27   T Robbins, 'Hour of Power – Start Your Day Like Tony Robbins' (20 June 2017), www.youtube.com/watch?v=a0B5vKp54HU, accessed April 2020

4.30am–6am: Thirty-minute Workout And Sixty-minute Walk

Having tried various workout schedules, working out at night and during the day, I found the most effective routine was to get moving first thing in the morning. As Tony Robbins states, 'The higher your energy level, the more efficient your body, the better you feel and the more you will use your talent to produce outstanding results.'[28] I learned that, to start my day off with success, I needed to have high energy to put into my work. This held me more accountable as there was nothing else that could come up throughout the day to eat into my workout time – no excuses.

6am–7am: Get Ready And Eat Breakfast

After a workout, I continue my morning ritual by having a shower, getting dressed and putting on my make-up as if I have an interview – even if no one will see me during the day, this makes me feel good about myself.

7am–11am: Four Hours Of Deep Work

I'm about to get super geeky and tell you about the one principle that changed my life and that is deep

---

28 Tony Robbins, 'Wheel of Life',
    http://core.tonyrobbins.com/wheel-of-life-4, accessed April 2020

work. I learned more about the concept from one of my favourite books – Cal Newport's *Deep Work* – but I had been practising deep work within my business for years without labelling it. In Cal's words:

> 'Deep work is the ability to focus without distraction on a cognitively demanding task. It's a skill that allows you to quickly master complicated information and produce better results in less time. Deep work will make you better at what you do and provide the sense of true fulfilment that comes from craftsmanship.'[29]

I have always been a deep worker, priding myself on abnormal levels of work within short time periods, without any interruptions. Most work that I complete requires a high level of concentration and creativity so I didn't think twice about practising deep work within my life. When my business began to have many moving parts to it and I was wearing all the hats, I realised I had started to lose my practice of deep work. I didn't realise how badly this impacted my level of concentration until I could no longer carry out a task without being distracted. I had formed a terrible habit of unlocking my iPhone and found that my thumb was automatically clicking onto my Instagram account. I would find myself unconsciously scrolling through my

---

29 C Newport, *Deep Work: Rules For Focused Success In A Distracted World* (Grand Central Publishing, 2016)

feed for no reason. I knew this had to stop, and soon. I had been losing hours each day that I could have been committing to growing my business. How do you run a business as a solopreneur, get everything completed and still crush your goals?

Managing Productivity

Prioritise What Is Important

If you follow me on social media, you've most likely heard me talking about 'needle-moving activities' (about which more below). Every business has different tasks to complete. Some of these may be admin tasks that need to be completed but other tasks and projects are going to take us closer to our goals. Where most entrepreneurs fail is spending too much time on the tasks that are taking them nowhere. 'Liv, that's really hard as I'm just starting out, it's just me.' I hear you – I was in the exact same position as you and I did it. But how?

Brain Dump

Identifying what is going to be a needle-mover in your business is going to help a lot. I practise a weekly and daily 'brain dump' or a 'brainstorm'. I open a new page in my diary and I just write anything that comes into my mind. Running several businesses can take its toll on your memory. I write down everything in my life that I need to complete. Even 'text brother about concert tickets' goes on there.

Needle-moving Activity

This is a task that will take your business a step closer to your goal. This is often a longer task, for example 'create webinar for online course launch'. These activities can often require two to eight hours of working time. These immediately take precedence every day. Perform needle-moving activities during hours of deep work; this is the most creative time that you can dedicate to propel your business forward.

Admin

An admin task is a boring task. This may be replying to emails, updating a system of processes within your company playbook or paying an invoice. If you aren't in a financial position to outsource admin, perform these activities in your dead time (outside the hours of deep work). This can also look like short sharp bursts of time between appointments or calls. These tasks need to be completed but they are mindless.

Delay And Delete

Being ruthless with your list is imperative to avoid overwhelm. I am guilty of focusing on tasks that aren't due for three months – just don't tell my team that. Why? These are low pressure tasks that help take your mind off the harder 'frogs' (I'll explain). Delaying them until closer to their due date can reduce overwhelm and allows you to focus on what is important now.

Eat The Frogs First

I love a to-do list. I love writing tasks on there that I've already completed just to feel more accomplished – I know you do it too. But at the end of the day the task I dread doing is still there. These are the frogs. You're never going to do it unless you do it first. As Tony Robbins says: 'If you talk about it, it's a dream, if you envision it, it's possible, but if you schedule it, it's real.'[30]

Schedule It

If it's not in the diary, does it even exist? Once I have prioritised my outcomes for the week, I schedule them into my diary and specify when each task will be complete. I focus on three main tasks each day, with my lower priority tasks being scheduled into dead time or being pushed back if not urgent.

---

30 T Robbins (@TonyRobbins), 'If you talk about it…'(12 July 2017), https://twitter.com/tonyrobbins/status/884933579461054464?lang =en, accessed April 2020

Go Extreme

I'm an extreme kind of girl – you might know that by now. It's all or nothing, black or white, I don't often see grey. Which means I'm a big picture thinker. Being like this is both a curse and a blessing, and I tend to implement extreme measures to get results. Like JK Rowling checking into a suite at the Balmoral (a five-star hotel in Scotland) for weeks to finish her final Harry Potter book,[31] or Bill Gates taking 'think weeks' where he disconnects from the world,[32] I often take off for days at a time to a hotel to work on a project, alone and uninterrupted. Completely shaking up your routine (ironic, given I just championed having one), can create some of your best and most creative work. It's an added pressure and negates distraction to enable you to complete the project at hand.

Challenge Yourself

In the same vein as getting away, changing your work location can help. I tend to find when working alone and with my team members that setting unrealistic

---

31 C Liao, 'Room of the Week: The J.K. Rowling Suite at The Balmoral in Edinburgh, Scotland', RobbReport (18 March 2019), https://robbreport.com/travel/hotels/the-balmoral-j-k-rowling-suite-harry-potter-references-2844202, accessed April 2020

32 J Hayes II, 'In the 1980s, Bill Gates would escape to secret cabin in the woods to protect himself from burnout. Here's the modern-day, easier version of his approach', BusinessInsider (2 August 2019), www.businessinsider.com/bill-gates-took-think-weeks-the-1980s-launched-internet-explorer-2019-8?r=US&IR=T, accessed April 2020

timescales for projects and tasks works. Such as setting a five-day goal for my podcast manager to launch a podcast, release five sixty-minute episodes and top the charts (we did it!), or when I set myself the task of creating my Thought Leader Accelerator online course in the space of five days, including 1,800 slides, 95 videos and 98 workbooks. I did it. Just remember, I have the same hours in a day as you and anything is possible.

Find A Unicorn

Transitioning from solopreneur to having the resources to outsource has pros and cons. I have experienced many struggles throughout my time in business and nothing has been more challenging than managing a team. Transitioning from everything being under your control and your responsibility to entrusting someone else with vital tasks in your business is a hard pill to swallow. Especially for someone like me, a perfectionist and a control freak (a bad combination as a manager or delegator).

The first hire in your business is a unicorn. A unicorn is a mythical creature, someone amazing who is rare or hard to catch.

When you are looking for your first hire you are looking for someone who can wear all the hats for you, to enable you to invest time into the needle-moving activities required for growing the business. You are basically looking for a clone of you but without the entrepreneurial flair, otherwise they'd be running their own start-up. They aren't easy to come by but I'm going to help you spot one.

You're already following my productivity hacks – great! What I'm going to share here is one of the best. I get shivers thinking about how productive this is. I wish someone had told me about this when I was looking for my first hire, it would have saved me many tears. Here's how to start:

- List all the tasks you are completing each day (no matter how small or big).

- Highlight anything you are completing which you feel doesn't have to be completed by you (these are your admin tasks, or something you feel you could teach someone else to complete).

- Do this from day one until you are ready to hire and keep in a document.

Voila, it's that simple: you have your first job description for your unicorn. There are a few things to bear in mind about the person you're looking for.

Look For A Jack Of All Trades

As you know, I value being the master in one subject, one industry and one platform. However, you want your unicorn to be good at most things. When interviewing and searching for your perfect candidate, hand them the list above and check they have experience with all the platforms you use.

They Won't Be With You Forever

Your unicorn most likely won't be with you forever. But why, you ask? Shouldn't they be loyal as they are employee number one? Yes, but a unicorn usually enjoys variety. They are the type of person who enjoys the chaos of a start-up. When you are out of the chaotic period of hustling, they will look for the next burning building to go extinguish.

They May Have A Slightly Quirky Set Up

The unicorns I have found don't usually have a traditional set up. For example, they aren't looking for a cookie cutter nine-to-five employed position. They usually have other things on the go, such as being a virtual assistant for other brands, or they have a family that they want to be flexible around. I say roll with it – if they are perfect for you, you'll come to an arrangement and work it out.

As entrepreneurs, we aren't always the easiest people to work with. From experience (and feedback), I know that I can be a challenging manager and teammate. It's hard to hear 'you aren't actually that great at this'. It's important to remember that your business is your baby and you steer the ship. You know the direction you want to head in; the challenge is enrolling your team into that same mindset and goal.

13

Your Circle

The motivational speaker Jim Rohn says: 'You are the average of the five people you spend the most time with.'[33] This is my favourite quote and it's one that I embody. Having been bullied for five years of my school life, I've experienced first-hand the impact of having the wrong people around you. Fortunately, I've learned that when you have the right people to elevate, support and inspire you, you can do anything.

---

33   A Groth, 'You're the average of the five people you spend the most
     time with', BusinessInsider (24 July 2012), www.businessinsider.com
     /jim-rohn-youre-the-average-of-the-five-people-you-spend-the-most
     -time-with-2012-7, accessed April 2020

I first began to embody the statement above when I had just started my business. I'd left school and none of my friends were like me – they were either still at school or heading to university so it was only natural that we drifted apart as I entered the crazy world of business. Partying until the early hours of the morning and going out on school nights just doesn't suit a young entrepreneur. I was going to bed at 8pm and waking at 4am, working sixteen-hour days Monday to Sunday. My friends couldn't understand why I wanted to work every hour of the day to realise my dream. Why couldn't I just be 'young and free'? I was, I was just doing it in my own way. The feeling of not belonging came flooding back and I knew I had to find my tribe, those who really understood me. As Steve Harvey said, 'You can't tell big dreams to small-minded people.'[34] I'm not saying my friends were small-minded, it was more that the pool of people who were speaking my language and understood me was small.

The Wrong People

How do you deal with those who aren't supporting your dreams? I've come up against challenging characters my entire life, as you do when you're going against the norm and your dreams are as big as yours

---

[34] S Harvey, 'Stop Telling Your Big Dreams to Small-Minded People', YouTube (3 September 2014), https://youtu.be/_5OqUnguixQ, accessed April 2020

and mine (and you're young). There is always going to be an element of 'who do you think you are?' from the wrong kind of person. I remember vividly the occasion when it was most obvious.

I had just done an interview with BBC Radio London and was heading to an awards ceremony afterwards. I was on a complete high from the interview. I got in the lift and a woman started to speak: 'Oh, I know you. Let me give you some advice, don't get too big for your boots.'

Wow! What a way to kill the buzz. It's a phrase that's used to mean: don't shine too brightly and don't forget where you came from. It really got me thinking. I was in shock that a stranger who didn't know me thought it was appropriate to say something like that. For the first time, I was met face on by the reason most people give up or don't even start. They are in fear of what someone else may think or, worse, what they'll say to your face. It's why I chose this title for the book; it's been a consistent theme throughout my journey. We live in a society in which it's frowned upon to be successful. Keep quiet and 'toe the line'. Don't be 'too successful' and certainly don't shout about it. To hell with that. Let your success be your noise.

The Right People

Taking a few moments, write down the five people you spend the most time with and evaluate:

- Who are they to me (coach, friend, family member)?

- How much time do I spend with them?

- What are the feelings I have when they are around?

- Are they supportive of my dreams and goals?

- Do they believe in me?

- Are they more successful than me?

It sounds so simple when someone says, 'You should only have the right people around you.' I understand that achieving this is challenging, especially when you're younger. Where do you meet these people? At this age the people you have around you will be those you've known since childhood, mainly school friends and family.

What did I do? I got networking and I created my own 'circle of trust', as described by Robert De Niro in *Meet The Fockers*.[35] Needless to say, the woman in the lift wasn't invited. How do we define your circle (or your

---

35   J Roach, *Meet The Fockers* [film] (Universal Pictures, 2004)

squad, or your tribe)? Let's be nerdy and check the dictionary definition of 'tribe': 'A group of people, or a community with similar values or interests.'[36]

Too official, let's change that up: 'Your unapologetically ambitious gang of badasses who are wildly supportive of your crazy dreams and goals.'

That sounds better. My circle of trust quickly started to include other entrepreneurs and business owners. People I could relate to. Just because you are building your tribe, that doesn't mean that we won't be approached in lifts or receive DMs online. How do we cope with the naysayers? Haters gonna hate, baby.

I want you to remember: you'll never be judged by someone more successful than you. Think of it logically – is Beyonce going be sliding into the DMs telling you to dim your light and stop marketing your business? Hell, no. Is Oprah Winfrey going to comment on your Instagram post telling you that your bum looks fat? Hell, no.

The only people with time to judge are those with nothing better to do and they are not invited into the circle of trust. My personal favourite is that big button available to us all. It's called 'block'. Both in real life and online, I'll hit it as many times as I need to. You don't need that kind of people in your life and you have the

---

36 www.yourdictionary.com/tribe, accessed 14 April 2020

choice to remove them. The other important thing to remember is that if someone takes issue with you it's not your problem, it's theirs. It's their insecurity – don't own it as if it's your own.

One of the perks of being an entrepreneur and one of the driving forces for me becoming my own boss was the freedom to decide who I get to work with. You remember my signature and my biggest social media fan is my mum. I knew immediately when my business started to grow that she was who I wanted to work with. Around two years in she decided to leave her business to join me and the rest is history. I trust her completely. One of my favourite questions, and one that I'm asked regularly, is: 'Is this your mum's business?' Step aside, my mum joined me and she's so proud of that fact.

Discovering whether you are a lone wolf or are looking for a business bestie to become a co-founder upfront is a vital step in the process. I have always worked better on my own, practising deep work. However, when it comes to strategising, growing the business and feeling there is someone in it with you, two heads are better than one. Whether you are a creative or a logical thinker (few people are both), there is always a gap to fill and you can do this with a co-founder. I'm a creative and I love innovating, but when it comes to finances, processes and people management I often lose interest in the implementation – cue my mum.

Finding a business partner isn't only good for business growth. Solopreneurship is a lonely path and there is a certain attraction to being 'in it together'. If you lose, you lose together. If you win, it's double the joy. My mum and I have a unicorn partnership; most mothers and daughters wouldn't be able to work together every minute of the day, or so I've been told. But beware: 62% of start-ups fail due to co-founder conflicts.[37] We aren't there yet. Years on and we have spent every day together and we are both still alive. Oh, I'm only playing. We make an amazing team.

Managing Successfully

My five years in business have given me massive insight into managing a team, especially as a young entrepreneur. We must possess a unique array of skills, especially managing employees older than us. Trying to plug the age gap has been one of the biggest challenges. How do you demand the respect of someone who is five, ten or twenty years your senior? I've had the classics: 'I have a pair of trousers older than you,' or, 'I won't be taking direction from you, *Missy*.' How do you:

---

37   J Burbank, 'Common Startup Co-Founder Mistakes and How to Avoid Them', Founder Institute (25 July 2016), https://fi.co/insight/common-startup-co-founder-mistakes-and -how-to-avoid-them, accessed 10 April 2020

- Prevent age being an issue?

- Deal with conflict when it arises?

As I've mentioned in my previous chapters, the best way to approach age is to deal with it head on. I address my age in the first interview. How you present to a potential employee is similar to how you brand yourself and your business. Position what you have already achieved with the business and a brief overview of the trajectory the business is taking and the potential role they will have in it. Then ask: 'How do you feel taking direction from me?'

Appreciate and use the other person's skills. With my mum, this would best sum us up: 'I create the magic and she edits it.' I have a creative brain but my editing skills can't compete with hers. Understanding where your team members' skills lie will save you not only conflict but also time and will advance your business at record speed.

Hiring Golden Rules

Building a team is the one thing I've struggled with. However, at twenty-one I've learned a thing or two. I hired my first employee when I was only eighteen; she was thirty-four years older than me. Trust me when I say I've dealt with all the issues when it comes to hiring a team and I want to share some golden rules with you.

Enrol Your Team In Your Vision

This is vitally important. No matter what role someone is playing in your business you need to ensure everyone knows not only the 'what' but also the 'why'. The why is what will motivate your team to go the extra mile to ensure success. When I was building my team, I hosted regular meetings and took everyone through the story of how the business got to where it was. In the case of ThePropertyStagers I would show everyone our first installation (which was awful, as were the next few) and show them the quality of what we were producing now. I would put up a slide show of the car I drove, the furniture packed in until I couldn't move. Why? To show them the journey, the hard work and sacrifice that had got me and the company to this point. I wanted their buy-in.

Customer service is a huge pillar in our business and I am always stressing its importance. A terrific way of demonstrating this was hosting our team meetings in a top-class hotel with impeccable customer service. We used the service delivery as an example and at the end of the meeting asked the team how we (the management team) and the hotel had made them feel. This was a powerful display of how we wanted to make our customers feel.

After you have hired your first employee, the task becomes more difficult as you now have more people in your team who need to 'fit in' with you and your first team member. However, depending on their role, there may not be a lot of interaction.

Don't Hire Someone Because You'd Like A Best Friend

One of the biggest mistakes I see young entrepreneurs making, and that I made, is hiring a new best friend. I often forewent the best candidate because I immediately 'clicked' with someone. They didn't have the skills that I needed at the time so we just didn't click in business and it didn't end in high fives.

Gain Respect As A Young Boss

This isn't easy but it is achievable. One of the most significant hurdles young leaders face, before they get the trust of those they are leading, is gaining the respect of your team. Face it head on. Acknowledge that you may be younger than anyone in the room but that the business is your brainchild, you have big plans and you want everyone to be a part of it. People want to be led by someone they trust who has a strong vision of where the business is heading and who can make the business they're working for successful. That's you.

You will gain respect by demonstrating your expertise in your industry, sharing your knowledge and empowering your team to make decisions – earn trust by giving trust. While demonstrating these attributes may not be easy, they provide a robust framework to getting you on the path to becoming respected as a young boss.

14
Coaching For Success

Iconic basketball player Michael Jordan is credited with saying, 'A coach is someone that sees beyond your limits and guides you to greatness.' Every time you reach a summit, there is always going to be another one waiting for you. Would you try to climb Mount Everest by yourself? If you did, it would take you twice as long, if you even made it. Business is much the same. Every time I have reached a summit, there has been a much bigger, steeper one that I have no clue how to reach.

This is called the 'what's next?' syndrome. You know what I mean. Of course you do – you are unapologetically ambitious, like me.

Every time I've reached that summit, I've looked for the right guide who's already been up to the next one. They've got the equipment, the tools, the map and they know the shortcuts. Why would I try to do it any other way? Yes, it might not have an upfront cost to do it alone, but it's going to take me longer (my time is money) and in the long run it will cost me a lot more money. Hey, it's a lot more expensive to pay for an emergency helicopter than it is to get to the next peak and back down safely.

Obviously you know I'm not talking about a mountain; it's a metaphor for business. I have climbed a few real mountains in my life, Ben Nevis being the most difficult one but so worth it. The view from the top was incredible and the sense of achievement was fun. Plus, each time I've reached the top, I wanted to do it again. Is there a pattern forming? I attribute the success I've had to a few factors, which I've covered throughout the book. The speed with which I've managed to achieve success has come through surrounding myself with the right coaches, who have been exactly where I want to go.

I've worked with coaches a few steps ahead of me to coaches with two million followers and eight-figure businesses. Those who I've been able to relate to most are the ones that started in the same circumstances I've come from. Paying to attend a large conference along-side 5,000 other people will motivate you and pump you up, but can the speaker relate to what it takes to build a business from ten followers when that's so far removed from their reality? Working with a coach who has walked the path you are on, and working with them in the right capacity, is the secret to a successful coaching relationship. I have worked in all capacities with coaches, so my insight should provide you with suggestions for what to look for yourself.

Types Of Coaching

Online Courses

Some of the best value content and learning I have consumed has been through online courses. The pro is that it's a lower entry price than working with a coach. However, the con is that you'll have to be a self-starter and disciplined as there is usually no form of accountability.

Perfect for: those with limited funds, looking to work through a programme at their own pace.

Live Events

Attending a live event is an incredible way to super-charge your energy and motivation, but you must take action when the event is finished. Speaking from experience, after attending Tony Robbins' Business Mastery event with 5,000 people in attendance, I increased my business by 400% in sales the following month. I am an action-taker and I implemented many of the strategies I learned from this event. Would the event have been as beneficial if I was a different personality type? Inspiration after a live event can die out quickly. Consider whether you need specific advice on your current business, as events usually do not include that – they are general.

Perfect for: those looking for a shot of adrenaline, creativity and motivation into their businesses and life.

Mastermind Or Group Coaching

A mastermind is usually undertaken with a group of people and is completed in a three-to-six-month timeframe. You will have one to three leading coaches who deliver the coaching material with a group of fellow mentees, usually between five and fifty people. I've been part of high paid masterminds (one with fifty people) and this structure didn't work well for me due to the speed of implementation. I was quickly ahead of the curriculum and I learn better in a solo setting.

Perfect for: those who are looking for a slower-paced curriculum, without the same accountability as one-to-one coaching; those who enjoy working alongside others and in a group setting.

One-to-one Coaching

Usually, this is the highest investment package, mostly because you have the undivided attention of one individual focusing on you and your business. The power of having a coach's eyes on your business is invaluable. Often, one recommended pivot from your coach can see you making your investment back quickly. I've experienced the greatest results when working solely with a one-to-one coach and now only consider working this way.

Perfect for: someone looking to make moves in their business at an accelerated pace, dedicated to business and personal growth.

What I Look For In A Coach

Understanding how you learn best is vital to building a successful relationship with your coach and choosing the right programme. Before choosing a coach, I consider what my ROI will be and how quickly it will come. Most importantly, I check in with the most powerful tool we have as entrepreneurs: my gut. Having worked with coaches who have changed my life, and some who have been the wrong fit for me, I've learned the hard and painful lesson of not trusting my gut. Those that didn't work out were the ones where my initial feelings were off. As with everything in business, when choosing a programme, whether it's an online course or a one-to-one coaching arrangement, always check to see if your coach aligns with your values. These are the factors I look for.

Transparency

This is vital, even if it risks us working together. I say to my potential coaching clients, 'Let's jump on a call to see if you like me and I like you.' There hasn't been a potential coaching client I haven't liked, but there have been clients I have suggested work with someone else. Coaching is a sacred relationship – the responsibility is on you, the mentee, to take action and get results. Nonetheless, a coach should only be working with you if they truly believe they can empower you to grow. I worked with one coach who should never have taken me on as a client, upon reflection. They didn't have the expertise to guide me on the subject I was looking to be coached on. I had to terminate our coaching package as it was draining my energy and finances for a poor service. That 'coach' attempted to take me to court. They should have turned me away at the point of consultation, as they couldn't help me. Be careful.

They Tell It To You Straight

Being on the other side of the conversation as a coach, it is fun to provide you with insights from both sides. When a client is looking to work with me as their coach, I take a realistic view of where they are now and what I think is possible. I've been promised as a mentee in the past that my income will triple in the space of a month. The coach obviously thinks that's what I want to hear but it's totally unrealistic. Be aware that you are receiving a realistic view of where you are, as starting a coaching relationship with unrealistic expectations creates an unhappy client.

They've Walked The Walk

Your coach has achieved what you would like to. This isn't always industry specific. In the education industry, I often see entrepreneurs signing up with coaches who haven't been where they want to go. If you want to become a seven-figure entrepreneur, you shouldn't work with a coach who has only hit the six-figure mark. Make educated decisions – only those who have been there can provide you with the map on how to join them.

They Care

It might be pointing out the obvious but, having worked with coaches who care about my business as much as theirs as well as those who blow off your coaching call for their own new product launch or exotic trips abroad, I know a bit about spotting a coach who is going to show up. One of my questions when considering a coach is: 'How much time will you be dedicating to our coaching together on a monthly basis?' Never forget that you are the client. Impostor syndrome, step aside.

What Is Their Story?

Always find out upfront. I worked with a coach who had amassed millions of followers on social media, had a large budget each month for advertising online and had received investment to get their business off the ground. I had launched my business with my pocket money and had zero social media followers when I launched. At the point of working together, I had few resources as investing in the coaching had drained any available funds I had to grow the business through paid strategies. I believed working together would elevate me to that next level. I was shown strategies to grow that were simply out of my reach. I didn't have millions of eyes on my content each month and I didn't have any funds for extravagant ad spend. They recommended outsourcing marketing to companies who often charged five figures per month. I had to be resourceful to get to where I wanted to go but my coach had never experienced this.

Researching what strategies your mentor has succeeded with is vital when it comes to working together successfully. Do they have applicable strategies to suit you if you have three followers or is it only applicable to their millions? As John Wooden says, 'A good coach can change a game, a great coach can change your life.'[38]

In a world where there is so much free content, how do we separate what we should be consuming for free and what we should be investing in? As an entrepreneur who creates endless free resources for my audience, I encourage my clients to always share their best content for free. Wait, why would I work with you for £10,000 then? With every business, brand and coach there is a ceiling to how much value you can receive for free. It's only fair – if we gave everything away for free then we would have no business. You'll begin to notice with free content that you get the what, not the how. Content creators are like magicians. They create content that will provide you with a certain level of knowledge which, if you are resourceful enough and you can read between the lines, you can implement yourself. However, they leave you wanting more, especially as

---

38   K Stolt, 'Why Coaches Matter', Medium (12 February 2018),
     https://medium.com/@MaxStolt/why-coaches-matter-6a11ed0bf302,
     22 April 2020

the majority of consumers aren't capable or determined enough to do the research.

Choosing A Coach

These are the three levels of investment:

1. Do it yourself

   - Price point: £

   - Usually an online course or event that you work through at your own pace, holding yourself accountable.

2. Do it with you

   - Price point: ££

   - Usually one-to-one coaching. Your coach's eyes are on your business but you are required to take joint or individual action to progress.

3. Do it for you

   - Price point: £££

   - Usually a one-to-one coaching package with an element of services carried out, such as online funnel building or managing your marketing or team. It could also include a two-day focused in-person mastermind.

The secret to your successful coaching relationship is in choosing the right mentor and being clear what the expectations are from both sides. Regardless of which form of coaching you invest in, the only person accountable for your own success is you. Success looks different for each person. Defining what success looks like is important; how can we measure our own success if we don't know what success looks like? Success isn't only financial, and I like to measure several main areas for both my personal happiness and business success.

How I Measure Success

Lifestyle

Having hustled for the first three years running my business, I know what having no lifestyle looks like: eighteen hours per day, seven days a week. Although I was achieving my business and financial goals, I had little fulfilment. I now measure my lifestyle goals in terms of:

- How do I feel, health-wise? Am I feeling fit and energetic?

- How often am I exercising?

- How is my work/life balance?

- Have I developed personally? What have been the lessons?

- How much time am I spending doing something I love (such as playing guitar)?

- How much time am I investing in people I love?

- What am I grateful for?

Business

Business growth isn't solely income based. Every month we track how we've grown our audience, our product launches, our back-end systemisation and organisation, our client impact, our team fulfilment and our team accountability:

- Did we do everything we committed to?

- What was our audience growth?

- Did we systemise or track our processes?

- What impact did we have on our clients?

- How is the team (including me) feeling?

- How can we improve as a team?

Finances

Having optics on my finances has been one of the biggest challenges I have faced as an entrepreneur. I'm a detail-oriented person but I'm not analytical (a little weird for a Virgo). I love setting financial goals but managing them has been tricky:

- Where are we currently – did we achieve last month's goal?

- What is our goal for next month?

- How much did we spend?

- What are our sales figures?

- How much profit have we made?

- Where can we tighten up?

Impact

'Your greatness is not what you have, but in what you give.'[39] This quote by Alice Hocker spoke to me and resulted in an initiative I launched in 2018 when I realised that we weren't having an impact on our community or helping those less fortunate. I launched the 100 Home Christmas Makeover, where we provide home transformations for those in low-income households or temporary accommodation at Christmas. We carried out these makeovers across Glasgow and London with support from some of the UK's biggest retailers such as M&S, Dunelm and Sainsbury's. The response was

---

39 I am Alice, 'Quote Worthy', https://alicehocker.com/quote-worthy, accessed 26 April 2020

so overwhelming that we have continued the initiative every year since.

Your 'impact' doesn't have to be huge, and we often support local businesses. Just recently we purchased 100 toothbrushes from BambuuBrush to give away to our social media following. We love this London-based company, founded by fellow entrepreneur Tommie Eaton, as they are trying to eliminate the amount of plastic products we use. Or you can go big, like we have with the launch of this book. My mission is to positively impact the lives of one million young people over the next year. It's ambitious, but it's possible with the right partners on board.

We ask ourselves these questions in a mini review at the end of every month, and a larger review at the end of every quarter, to keep on track:

- Have we made an impact on our clients this month?

- Have we made an impact on the community?

- Have I personally made an impact on anyone's life?

It can often feel like a hassle to carry out such reviews but if you don't track the numbers then how can you work out your return on investment? Holding yourself accountable for results and implementation is vital to your success.

15
Next Level

What's next? Your next level. In every business, including mine, there comes a moment when you realise that you are ready to step things up a notch. As ambitious entrepreneurs, it's when we've hit our seemingly impossible goal. But once we've smashed it, we want to conquer the next one.

This feeling hit me when I had just won my first business award. I was recognised in my industry for the 'best product of the year' in our home staging service. It was an indication that this was the time to capitalise on what we were doing. We were featured in the newspaper for the first time and then started building momentum. Within twelve months of winning our first award we won a further nine international business and entrepreneurial awards. I was flown across the world to speak at prestigious international events, I was named the UK Young Entrepreneur of the Year at twenty and I received opportunities that few people my age could dream of. I became a thought leader in my space.

Every time I've reached the next level, I've looked for the expert who is already there. It's been the one thing that has propelled my business forward but it didn't happen overnight. Quite the opposite. I've never relied on anyone to take me there, but they guided me along the way. You may be reading this book and thinking, 'I wish I could be where Liv is at twenty-one.' I felt the *Exact* same when I looked at other successful people, but they are on their Chapter 10 and I'm still only on my Chapter 2. It's all to come for you. Plus, your role models still have the exact same feelings as you.

Anything Is Possible

I was in Los Angeles on business when an email arrived in my inbox from 10 Downing Street, inviting me to dinner with the Prime Minister on Burns Night. Talk about impostor syndrome. My initial reaction was that it must be a scam – why would they invite me? I sent it on to a contact who might be able to tell whether it was real or not. Not only was it real, but I had been asked to give the Address to the Haggis (I suggest you

Google that). From the outside looking in, my life has become a highlight reel of incredible moments, but it didn't happen overnight.

It took hustle and a combination of consistency, resilience and a will to never give up. I made sacrifices and took risks. I bet on myself that this is what I was meant to do. Waking up at 3am to drive for six hours to London to stage a property and then drive back the same day. The countless late nights staging properties until 2am and showing up on social media with a smile on my face after eighteen-hour shifts. Unloading vans of furniture in the pouring rain (and snow) to get the job done. Properties I locked myself out of and wiped away my profit paying a locksmith to get me back into so I didn't have to bother the client. Falling up and down countless staircases, carrying boxes heavier than my body weight, getting changed in bathrooms at networking events and showing up even though I was exhausted and didn't have a clue where I was going. The moments crying in my car, questioning if I could really do this – should I just go and get a job? The obsession I felt was powerful, a determination and fire to prove every doubter wrong and build this into a wildly successful business. What is done in the dark is seen in the light and soon you'll be given the spotlight you deserve.

Everything we have discussed in this book has provided you with the tools to become a thought leader.

However, if you are reading this and you haven't yet built the business, that's OK. I like to call it pre-emptive learning; you're gaining valuable knowledge before you need it. I didn't implement some of these strategies until I had been in business for a few years. Now is the time to lay the foundations. Let's not think small – supersize it. I want you to think international. I can tell you through my own experience that anything is possible. The secret isn't in thinking, 'I can't,' but rather in asking, 'How can I?' Always lead with the solution. There is nothing that is out of your reach. Get rid of your inner critic, it's only holding you back. Let's go big.

Becoming A Thought Leader

Thought leaders are the informed opinion leaders and the go-to people in their field of expertise. They are trusted sources who move and inspire people with innovative suggestions, turn ideas into reality and show you how to replicate their success.

To become a thought leader, experience and expertise within your industry aren't enough. Being recognised for your achievements and respected among peers is vital. We have discussed organic ways to grow your brand, such as offline marketing strategies and social media. However, if you want to add some fuel to the fire and create social proof, you'll need to raise your profile. The most effective way to do this is creating powerful partnerships with the right people, winning awards and being featured in the press.

The one thing you can do today to propel your personal brand is align yourself with the right people and businesses. Once you understand how to leverage someone else's audience, thought leadership and respect throughout the industry start to quickly build momentum. Reputation can take years to build and minutes to destroy. Choosing an aligned partnership (just like choosing a coach) is incredibly important for your success. How can we recognise an aligned partnership?

Define Your Values

Values are the most important thing to any entrepreneur or organisation. They serve as a compass that guides you on your journey (you know I love a metaphor around navigation). Choosing your values will keep you on track and help with the big decisions in your business, especially when you have become a leader in your space and you are trying to protect your reputation.

I'm a big fan of finding your circle, the right coach and the right person to take you to the next level, but the one thing I haven't shared with you is the people you will meet throughout your journey who could provide you with game-changing opportunities. I often get asked about the opportunities I've received. I have been invited to Downing Street, I've been interviewed by Karren Brady CBE and she invited me out for tea, I have won awards and I have been flown across the world to speak at events. You might be reading this and thinking: how on earth is that ever going to happen for me? I was in the exact same position as you, I couldn't have dreamed most of this up. I had no clue any of this would happen but it wasn't by accident.

I want to bring you full circle in conclusion to our time together and take you back to thirteen-year-old Liv who started her eBay business selling nails. I put myself out there, I lived outside my comfort zone and I went against the norms. Just like you are now. It's not easy but it's paid off. I still experience impostor syndrome and when I mention in this last chapter some of the opportunities I've had, I really can't believe that they are in the same sentence as my name. I say that with complete transparency. There is a currency that we have as young people, especially young entrepreneurs, and that is our fearlessness. It has guided me on my path and showed up every day of my life.

A fearlessness to not give a damn about what people say, what people think and a fearlessness to ask for what we want when we want it. We decide on our own timescales – age is literally a number. My biggest opportunities have come from being around the right people and being able to ask for help. It's something

I have always struggled with. My mum mentioned that my favourite saying is 'I'll do it myself' but, if we are being realistic, we can't do everything ourselves. Think of some of the most successful people in the world – they wouldn't have achieved half of it without the help of others.

Grab Opportunities With Both Hands

I'll let you in on a little secret before we reach the end of our time together. I asked Marc Randolph to do the Foreword for this book after I had interviewed him on my podcast. It was my brother who initially identified him and asked him on as a guest. I couldn't believe that my brother thought to aim so high or that Marc actually agreed (impostor syndrome, once again). I was sick to my stomach all day. I was so nervous as I pressed 'stop recording' on our Zoom call. I asked Marc for his valuable time to give back to young entrepreneurs by writing the Foreword for this book. You don't need to guess what he said, as you've already read it.

Had I not asked for Marc's help, or the countless other people I have asked for help in the creation of this book – my publishers, the editors, my agent, my mum and brother – I would be years behind where I am right now. We possess a special power as young entrepreneurs that I never want you to forget. Those who have walked the path before us want to give us a hand up. It took me a long time to realise it and to embrace it but, when I think back to most of the opportunities I've grabbed with both hands, they have all come from people who have read my story and connected with me. Never underestimate the power of your story.

I am so excited to connect with you, to see you step into where you belong and follow your dreams. There will be a second book in the pipeline for me to help you on the next steps of your journey. I know there's a reason you want to become an entrepreneur, and I know that because I have one too. There is an underlying desire in you. I can only describe it as a fire that has burned in the pit of my stomach ever since I was a child. Every day I do what I love just adds fuel to the fire. Your 'why' is the purpose, cause or belief that drives you. It's what makes you jump out of bed in the morning and it's what made you pick up this book. Business, unlike a lot of the world, isn't discriminatory. You don't have to be a certain age, race or gender or have a certain level of income to become successful. Business favours the innovators, the rule breakers, the risk takers and the hard workers. People just like you and me.

I wasn't sure how to start this book and I can't say I'm entirely sure how to end it either. I'm working it out as I go along. Sound familiar? Trust me when I say: as long as you never give up, anything is possible.

Afterword

Congratulations, you have finished the book and invested your time and energy to learn not only how you can build the business of your dreams, but how to live authentically as yourself in a world that isn't always accepting. However, as Marc mentioned in the Foreword, reading a book is just reading a book. It is in taking action where you will start to take strides forward and make an impact.

Although, there are many valuable chapters throughout the book, it is in your future chapters where the magic lies.

To support each of you in reaching your goals and become who you want to be, I've created many different resources and ways that I can continue to aid you on your journey.

Your Scorecard

Optics on where you are right now, this is the only tool that will enable you to move forward. My scorecard assesses your current strengths and areas of growth to focus on. It will give you a customised report and access to training videos.

Visit: www.TooBigForYourBootsBook.com/scorecard

Facebook Page

Join your tribe and the people who speak your language in our wonderful community for real time support, friendship, inspiration and updates.

Visit: www.facebook.com/groups
/theentrepreneurialcircle

Your Personal Brand Accelerator

Ready to take things to the next level? Hungry for wild success? My signature online programme is designed for the entrepreneur who wants more impact, influence and income.

Visit: www.TooBigForYourBootsBook.com/Accelerator

Acknowledgements

It's easy to forget that behind a successful entrepreneur there's usually a team that make it all possible.

I create the magic and she proofreads and edits it. I am of course talking about my incredible mum! Not only are you my mum, you're also my right-hand woman, my best friend and the business partner I couldn't do any of this without. Thank you, mum; I really wouldn't have written this book or had the success behind me to warrant a book without the support you give me every day.

To Jack, my amazing brother. Most siblings would struggle to work together but our daily zoom calls make me cry with laughter. You're not only the brains behind the book launch, without you I never would have secured a foreword by one of the world's most successful entrepreneurs. Jack, you have pushed me to dream bigger than I ever thought possible and creating this book together will always be one of my most cherished memories.

To Marc, it was the highlight of my career when you agreed to write the foreword. You are one of the most humble and gracious men I have had the pleasure of coming across. Your commitment to give back and inspire young people has truly moved me and I hope, in business and in life, I will follow in your footsteps and one day be able to pay it forward to someone else.

Mike Handcock and Landi Jac, without you, this book wouldn't actually be in your hands. You both have pushed me time and time again to the next level and forced me to think outside the box. You have been the most incredible mentors and will be friends for life.

To Daniel Priestley, for inspiring me to write a book that changed my life. I'm so appreciative of your continued support and for so generously introducing me to my publisher, thank you.

To my publisher, Rethink Press, in particular Joe Gregory who has spent countless hours on Zoom strategising how to make an impact; you have been so generous and patient. Also, a massive thank you to Eve Makepeace, my project manager, who has been there at every point we have needed her. This book really wouldn't be here without you both.

The Author

Many of the world's most successful ideas are born out of frustration, and twenty-one-year-old Liv Conlon's property staging business is no exception. Her first introduction to the world of business was when, aged thirteen, she began importing products from China and reselling them via eBay after school at a healthy profit.

When Liv's mum Ali struggled for several months to sell her investment property, Liv, then seventeen, had an epiphany. She knew about the concept of staging homes but couldn't find anyone who offered the service at an affordable price, so she decided to do it herself. It was a great success and ThePropertyStagers was born.

The company achieved a £1-million turnover in the first year. Currently operating throughout the UK, ThePropertyStagers and their team furnish around 300 properties each year.

Liv canned her early plans to go to university, instead leaving school aged seventeen without a business plan, determined that she would be her own boss. Today the young businesswoman is fast accruing a mantelpiece laden with business awards, eleven since 2019, including FSB UK Young Entrepreneur of the Year and five-time winner of the Young Scottish Business Person of the Year.

Beyond continued business growth, Liv's goal is simple – to share the message that there are alternatives to the traditional academic route and champion the notion of profit with purpose. To that end, she is currently part of the BBC Bitesize Project, which showcases inspirational stories of those who have overcome adversity – in Liv's case, being bullied at school. She explores the entrepreneurial mindset and highlights the value to the economy and broader society of young entrepreneurship.

Liv's passion for promoting profit with purpose led her to begin the 100 Home Christmas Makeover, which partners with charities and homeware companies to improve the lives of deprived families. She continues to inspire millennials to start their own businesses and blaze their own trail with a goal of positively impacting the lives of one million young people in the next year. She helps other entrepreneurs achieve similar levels of success through The Thought Leader Method™.

Liv often speaks on TV and radio as an entrepreneurial expert, regularly appearing on BBC News and ITV. She has spoken about building a seven-figure brand at a young age, overcoming bullying and how she went from being an unknown sixteen-year-old to an industry disruptor and leader.

🌐 livconlon.com
🅕 www.facebook.com/livconlon.co.uk
🅛 www.linkedin.com/in/liv-conlon-73a26bbb
🅧 https://twitter.com/oliviaconlon
🅘 www.instagram.com/oliviaconlon

Printed in Great Britain
by Amazon